Also by Sonny Kleinfield

A MONTH AT THE BRICKYARD

THE
HIDDEN
MINORITY

THE
HIDDEN
MINORITY

A Profile of Handicapped Americans

by Sonny Kleinfield

Introduction by Robert Coles

An Atlantic Monthly Press Book
LITTLE, BROWN AND COMPANY · BOSTON · TORONTO

FIRST EDITION

Portions of this book have appeared in *Psychology Today* and
The Atlantic.

LIBRARY OF CONGRESS CATALOGING IN PUBLICATION DATA

Kleinfield, Sonny.
   The hidden minority.

   "An Atlantic Monthly Press book."
   1. Physically handicapped — United States.
I. Title.
HV3023.A3K53   362.4'3'0973   79-14812
ISBN 0-316-49842-4

ATLANTIC—LITTLE, BROWN BOOKS
ARE PUBLISHED BY
LITTLE, BROWN AND COMPANY
IN ASSOCIATION WITH
THE ATLANTIC MONTHLY PRESS

BP

Published simultaneously in Canada
by Little, Brown & Company (Canada) Limited

PRINTED IN THE UNITED STATES OF AMERICA

For Bernice

Introduction

by Robert Coles

THE first work I did, as a child psychiatrist, was with
severely handicapped boys and girls — victims of paralytic
polio in the middle 1950s. In no time those children had
been transformed, by the hand of fate, from active, energetic
youngsters to a state of involuntary passivity. And soon
enough they would know that a vaccine had, for all practical
purposes, made them the last such American polio victims.
At that point in my life I was rather too strenuously interested in what was wrong — the psychopathology that a
young doctor goes hunting after and, given the nature of
all of us, finds in abundance. Forgetting the obvious — that
a handicapped child is, after all, a person with strengths as
well as vulnerabilities — I concentrated on the fears and
worries I took pains to elicit, in conversation, from the young
patients I was visiting. One day, however, a girl of ten
brought me up short. I was poking around, as usual — more
arrogant, blind, condescending than I apparently had any
way of knowing — when suddenly, in response to a not so
innocent inquiry (what were her plans for the future?) she
gave it to me: "I want to live my life! And I will!" I had in
my mind, of course, all the obstacles that lay ahead of her.
I was trying to get her to think of them, to be "realistic."

As if she hadn't been thinking of "them"! As if she wasn't, every minute of every day, quite insistently reminded by her eyes, by her particular experience of herself, what her body could and could not do!

I thought of her, and those (to me, unforgettable) words of hers as I read this important, powerfully written, quite touching book of Sonny Kleinfield's. When one of his friends, Hillam, declares that he is "leading a life," we are brought as close as anyone ever gets, maybe, to the essence of personal affirmation: the mind's will turned into an everyday kind of human actuality, against high and continuing odds. Throughout this book we meet such individuals, people whose struggle to "lead a life" ought to teach us that the stuff of heroism is nearby, indeed. The author also has a lot of important social and psychological observations to offer us; he gives the reader economic and political information — the way we as a nation regard those who aren't up to our conventional ideas of what a person ought to be able to do. Just as important, the author has a marvelously compelling manner of narrative presentation; he works his "data," his surprising and often saddening factual material, into the lives of particular men and women whom we get to know, and to whom, I suspect, a number of us will in our thoughts keep coming back.

Long ago an itinerant preacher drew upon His awesome healing powers, as He trekked the Middle East portion of the Roman Empire. Again and again He chose "the lame, the halt, the blind" as objects of His attention and compassion. He saw in them allies — people who, ironically, were kin to Him, all-powerful One that He was. He knew, too, that insofar as we hurt or ignore or reject those who are injured, suffering, we condemn ourselves to a far harsher exile than that experienced by "them." We show ourselves to be callous, smug, cold-hearted, high and mighty in our self-centeredness. And doing so, we take on a risk that may well be eternal as well as temporal in character. That is to say, we lose, concretely and here and now, the considerable human resources of mind and, yes, of body that thousands upon thousands of men and women have to offer America. But we also risk losing something else — our own dignity badly tarnished — both by emotional stinginess, and by a narrowness of vision that can only be called spiritual.

ROBERT COLES

THE
HIDDEN
MINORITY

1

Fighting heavy traffic, we rumbled onto the San Bernardino Expressway and headed through the darkness toward La Verne. A jetliner banked in the sky above us, squirted hydrocarbons, and lowered its flaps for Ontario Airport. We were riding in what had been intended as a Frito-Lay delivery truck. No chips were aboard, however, just us. The truck made quite a racket as it bumped along. Every crack in the road felt like a crevice, every pebble felt like a rock, and I spent a lot of my time reaching for the door handle to maintain my equilibrium. I was the passenger. The driver, Bruce Hillam, sat beside me in a wheelchair.

"The freeways are the easiest places to drive with hand controls," he said. "All you have to do is get up to fifty-five and swoop along. Tonight, I'm afraid, we'll have to swoop along at forty-five."

Miles came slowly in flat land, where the view from the cab — uninterrupted in every direction — ran over miniature golf courses, drive-in burgers, and a winding road on which small Grand Prix cars were thundering around curves. With light-edged contempt, Hillam refers to this neighborhood as "plastic country." Rain puddles glimmered along the edge of the road. "We've really had a ton of rain out here lately,"

Hillam said. "Rain may be pretty uncomfortable for you, but it's horrendous for me. The belts of my wheelchair get all soaked and it ends up squeaking constantly. Everyone knows when I'm coming."

"What do you do about it?" I asked.

"Stay out of the rain," Hillam said.

His paralysis begins at the nipples. Below, he is diminished. Above, in the arms and shoulders, Hillam is fairly able, though the fingers of each hand are locked together. The steering wheel of the truck has black slots that he fits his welded hands into in order to drive. Shaking hands with Hillam is a bit like shaking hands with a tree branch.

The miles peeled off soon enough, and we turned off the highway onto a narrow and dark side street. Hillam's truck seemed to more than span the width of the road. To the onlooker, it is almost offensively ungainly. Yet Hillam made the driving seem effortless, which he claimed it was. "It's a lot of bull that if you're handicapped you can't drive," he said. "The notion that there's so much we can't do is like an albatross around our necks. I've yet to cause any forty-car collisions." Mounted at the rear of Hillam's chair was a small ham radio for emergencies. Once he got a flat tire on the expressway and a full forty-five minutes passed before a car stopped. We shimmied onto Smokehouse Street, a tree-lined lane of low houses, and swung into Hillam's driveway. "You don't often see a nine-foot-tall garage like that, now do you?" he asked. I admitted that I didn't. He killed the engine and punched a switch that flung open the rear door of the truck. Shoulders seesawing, Hillam drove his motorized wheelchair onto a silver ledge, then touched another control that, with a wrenching noise, lowered the entire ledge down onto the ground. "Those are power switches off a Cadillac," he said. "Adds a little class to the truck."

A long wooden ramp led from the garage to the house. Five bags of steer manure were stacked next to it for future use in Hillam's garden. Hillam clacked up the ramp and into the kitchen. One of his two attendants, a clean, fresh college student named Dody, greeted us. The house was specially built for Hillam, since he couldn't find an existing home that suited his needs. The living and dining areas were one gaping space; the hallways were wide enough for a small vehicle to chug through. Instead of door knobs, levers were attached to all of the doors. Light switches were mounted low on the walls. The roof was made of cement. Two years ago, a brush fire ravaged thirty thousand acres of La Verne, and Hillam has since developed a strong fear of fire. In his bedroom, a mechanical lift reposed next to the bed, a stark reminder that both a machine and an attendant were needed to get him in and out of bed. Nothing else about the place was remarkable, other than the bathroom off Hillam's bedroom. It boasted a door that slid into the wall, for easy access, and a shower with no lip; instead, a sunken area had been built into the center to allow water to drain. "I had to go through all sorts of red tape to get that shower approved," Hillam said. "The rule is you've got to have a six-inch lip. Fine, but who's going to be Samson and carry me over? We haggled for weeks before the town said okay."

Awkwardly, Hillam creaked into the living room. He is a gregarious man, jowly, with a tumble of dark hair. A big man. I saw no suggestion of softness in his burly, broad-shouldered frame, and he has the biceps of an NFL line-backer. His face is weather-lined, handsome, and tough. His voice is fluid and melodic. Dody fetched us some tea. The TV was going, an old Cary Grant movie. Lots of smooching. Hillam sipped some tea and said, "So here you have Bruce Hillam, quadriplegic, living his own independent life like

Archie Bunker or anybody else. Just like Cary Grant, for that matter, except a little less womanizing for me. I have my ups and downs, but I'm leading a life. That's the important thing. I'm not warehoused in some institution. I'm not a vegetable that needs to be watered every two days. I'm leading a life."

September 9, 1961, was a hot, mucky day. Anybody with sense was at the beach. Bruce Hillam was a six-foot string-bean, fifteen years old, a high school freshman. His father was in the Marine Corps, so it was perfectly natural that Hillam had joined the Boy Scouts when he was small. Now he had climbed to the rank of Explorer Scout. As one of their good deeds, the Scouts picked litter off the beaches. So this Labor Day weekend found Hillam clearing Coors beer cans and crumpled hot dog wrappers off the Oceanside beach. Boring work. After a few hours of it, the Scouts fell into a game of follow the leader. One of them happened on a fifteen-foot-deep eddy pool. Adjacent to it was a sand bar. Perfect for diving, he figured. He dove in, daring the others to follow. Hillam loved to swim. During the summer, he had been a lifeguard. He was one of the first to follow.

He remembers hitting the water. Going under and floating back to the surface are not part of his conscious memory. The next thing he recalls is lying on the surface, head down, in a dead man's float. "I was saying to myself, 'Hey Bruce, why don't you turn over already? You've done this long enough.' You know what it's like when your arm falls asleep? That's how my whole body felt." Poised along the water's edge, his friends thought Hillam was horsing around. A batch of them swam over. "I said, 'Well I feel a little stunned, but I'll be all right in a minute.' Those were my famous first words." Hillam wasn't able to move. His friends dragged him onto the shore, and one of them called an ambulance.

"I had always wanted to drive an ambulance," Hillam would say later. "It was one of my childhood fantasies. Well, I came close. I was the passenger."

At the Camp Pendleton hospital, doctors pounded Hillam with a mallet and pricked him with a pin. He felt nothing. The fifth, sixth, and seventh vertebrae of his spinal cord had snapped, and nothing was going to put them back together. No neurosurgeons were on the staff at Camp Pendleton, so Hillam took another ambulance trip to the San Diego Naval Hospital. His mother met him there as he was being prepped for surgery. "The next thing I remembered was being cold — extremely cold. I was in the recovery room, and I'd have sworn it was thirty-two degrees in there. They had me in what's best described as a hot dog bed. Mattresses were above and below me, so they could flip me — the hot dog — every two hours and I wouldn't get bedsores. Jesus, I had a hard time getting used to that."

Hillam's father had been fishing in Fish Lake, Utah. He arrived the next day. "I remember him visiting me in my room," Hillam has said. "They shave all your hair off for this kind of operation. They had put it in a paper bag and stood it on the nightstand next to me, in the event I died. The mortician would still have something to glue back on. They had drilled some holes in my head. I imagine I was quite a preposterous sight."

Soon Hillam was transferred to an orthopedic hospital in Los Angeles. The first assault of depression that was to afflict him for some years had yet to set in. He had failed to accept the dark reality of his injury. "I was sure that I was going to beat this thing. I was sure that medical science being what it was, I would get up and walk out in due time. I might have to swallow a few pills, the doctor might have to snap his fingers, but I'd be walking soon." At the hospital, Hillam earned a reputation as a general pest. He would ride the elevators for hours, which irritated the nurses, who never knew where he was. Other times, he and friends in the ward would get together and flash mirrors into the nurses' faces.

The ugly truth came to Hillam in blunt and inescapable fashion. His ward was deep in paraplegics and quadriplegics, but he had no reason to believe that he and they wouldn't walk and dance again. "Then one day this black guy arrived, pretty young, paralyzed from an auto accident. When the doctors told him his condition, the guy said that with a broken neck he'd just be useless. He'd be a burden to his family and to society. Just let him die. Seven days later, he died. The doctors said he just lost the will to live." Almost immediately afterward, another man arrived; he had broken his neck after inadvertently driving off a cliff. He wanted to live so badly that he developed an ulcer and doctors had no choice but to remove his stomach to keep him alive. He died in a week. "So here I was, a sixteen-year-old kid, in a ward where one man had committed psychological suicide and another guy wanted to live so badly he worried himself to death. Other patients around me had had accidents like mine, and two or three years later they weren't walking. They weren't running. So I realized my problems were permanent. They weren't going to put me back together. The sun would shine tomorrow, but I still wouldn't walk. That's when I remember crying myself to sleep."

Fortunately for him, Hillam was part of an extremely close-knit family that showered him with constant support. What's more, he had a stubborn conviction that, no matter what, life was worth living, and he didn't intend to give up on it. "I generally kept up a good face. I realized pretty early in the game that if I was a real SOB I'd lose everything. My first doctor, who was a real pill, didn't even get me down. He told my parents that they ought to buy me a mynah bird or a lap dog, a TV and some records, because I'd probably want to stay in bed all the time. Not what you'd call the greatest bedside manner."

The prolonged process of physical therapy began. The time unrolled like a jerky and utterly unengrossing movie. "The real problem is learning how to use what you've got left. My fingers couldn't move. I had to relearn how to write. You write with your fingers and your wrists. I had to learn how to write with my shoulders. I started off with a four-foot letter. Physical therapy was incredibly, incredibly tiring. We began with this loom — a typical physical therapy thing — and one day I noticed they had put weight on my loom. So it was harder to pull up. I started playing checkers. One day, lo and behold, I noticed the checkers had weights on the bottom. Pretty sneaky."

Two years elapsed before Hillam left the hospital to return home for good. He had three sisters. Each took his tragedy well. "One accused me of breaking my neck to get out of doing the dishes. We used to alternate. My other sister accused me of doing the same thing, because she was stuck with taking over my dish duty. My third sister was four and was just curious. I told her I had gotten tired of walking and was trying a life of sitting."

Before too long, Hillam resumed school. He recalls arriving the first day — his mother drove him to and from school — and at the assembly welcoming back students the principal put in a long and passionate plug for him. Moved by it, the students and teachers in the audience responded with a standing ovation. He thought that was a bit much. "After all, I hadn't written the great American novel. I hadn't cured cancer." Most of Hillam's friends dropped deep into the background, since they were interested chiefly in physical activities that Hillam could no longer indulge in. For the balance of high school, Hillam's social life ground to a standstill.

More and more, he found himself transported into a somber and unfamiliar world. His sense of humor became increasingly specked with despair. "The handicapped person, I learned, didn't count for anything. I had been labeled one of life's losers." Sheer determination and strong family support got Hillam through high school, then college, where he eventually earned a Ph.D. in mathematics. He decided to become an industrial mathematician. "Most interviewers got more of a kick out of my electric wheelchair than they did out of me. Nobody was interested in hiring an obviously physically disabled person. I heard the usual litany of excuses: what about insurance rates? how would I get around? what would co-workers think with this freak in their midst?" Hillam finally rewrote his career plans and found a teaching job. He's now a professor of math and computer science at California State Polytechnic University. "Fellow professors generally regard me as one of them. The attitude in the academic world tends to be a bit more liberal than in the corporate world. Students are surprised and kind of uneasy when they first see me clack into the classroom at the beginning of a semester. There's always this background of murmuring. After a few weeks, though, they get the message that I can teach as well from a wheelchair as I can from my feet. You don't need feet to think."

The Cary Grant movie wound toward its conclusion. It was late, I had flown in from New York and was operating on a different time, so I said I was going to turn in. The plastic cushion on Hillam's wheelchair crinkled as he shifted to point out my room. Normally it was occupied by his other attendant, Kim, but tonight she was going to stay with her boyfriend. It was quite homey. "If you hear a loud buzzer in the middle of the night," Hillam said, "just ignore it. That's to wake Dody to turn me over so I don't get bedsores. If I get bedsores, I might have to spend five thousand dollars to get rid of them. I'd rather use the money for something else."

We polished off some orange juice in the morning. From a distance, the dining room table looked odd, for I saw no chair at its head. That was where Hillam sat. He had already done some work; he was writing a calculus textbook, his first and, judging from the difficulty he was having, he thinks perhaps his last. The day was already muggy, and would probably get worse. Hillam had on a plaid shirt and light brown seersucker pants. He had obviously just been shaved, because the pungent scent of a cologne wafted from him every time he moved.

To shave him and otherwise enable him to carve out an independent life, Hillam has always employed two part-time attendants. They alternate being on duty. Dody was on today. The basics of their assignment are to clean the house, do the laundry, cook two meals a day, and pack Hillam a bag lunch (Hillam does the food shopping himself, for he finds the bills are noticeably lower when he picks out the goods; when he can't reach something, he sits tight until someone passes by. Just recently the supermarket he patronizes finally widened one of its checkout aisles so that his wheelchair can slip through.) The attendants must get him out of bed in the morning, change his drainage bags, bathe him, and wrestle him into his clothes. At night, they undress him and put him to bed. Twice a week, they wash his hair. When Hillam goes out with company, he usually manages alone. One of the attendants, though, must accompany him when he heads out of town on a trip, and, when he goes clothes shopping, salesmen typically don't rush to help him try things on.

Hillam comes by his attendants by tacking ads on bulletin boards at the college campus ("Cal Poly prof in wheelchair will exchange room, board, and $100 a month for person to share the duties of a part-time live-in housekeeper aid. Hours are flexible and will not interfere with school"). He only hires students, since he can't afford the higher fees that career attendants require. Smokers are also out, because, being a quadriplegic, Hillam can only take about half a full breath, and he has a hard time clearing his lungs. Attendants have stayed with Hillam for as little as two weeks (one eloped, and another was axed when Hillam discovered she was a kleptomaniac who was robbing him blind) and as long as three years. Many handicapped people recruit full-time attendants through employment agencies, or the Easter Seal Society, or through other agencies that work with the disabled. As yet, no companies specialize in the field. A friend of Hillam's has retained an attendant for seventeen years, and another is marrying his. Not much training is required. Hillam told me he can train an attendant in just three days.

I asked Hillam to describe to me some of the forms of discrimination he has faced.

He gave this some thought, then said, "The problems, I can assure you, go well beyond the obvious ones of mounting stairs, reaching phones, using bathrooms, and squeezing through doors. Any ordinary chore can be an incredible nuisance. When I first came here, I wanted to see a movie. I think it was *Dirty Harry*. I had called the theater and was told it was accessible by wheelchair. I went down, paid my admission and parked my wheelchair in the rear of the theater. The manager hurried over and asked me if I could get out of my wheelchair. I said no. He asked me if I wanted help to get out of it. I said no. He told me I was a fire hazard if I stayed in the chair. We argued back and forth, and I said I wanted my money back. He refused and finally left me with an usher standing directly over my shoulder the entire time."

He threw one of his arms behind his head, as if he were about to release a forward pass, pondered a moment, chuckled, then went on.

"I've been in a restaurant and was seated in a banquet room by myself. I said, 'Gee, I'd kind of like to be in the other room with the rest of the people, it wasn't that crowded in there. I always wanted to be honored at a banquet, but it loses something without the audience.' The manager made this crack that, well, he didn't want the other customers to be frightened. I left. Once, I went to a restaurant with my sister. The waitress gave me a menu but only addressed my sister. She asked my sister what I'd like to have, as if I were a baby. When something like that happens, I leave a penny tip. When I go clothes shopping, I need someone to help me get things on. The salesperson will always address questions to that person: What size does he wear? Could he use some suspenders, too? As if I were a pet. Two or three times a year, I'm stopped by religious fanatics who insist that I'm not up and about because of my lack of faith in the Lord. Or by the types who urge me to just hang in there, God has big plans for me. I was Christmas shopping last year when this woman who looked like a grandmother's grandmother came up to me and, before I could get out a word, she had her hands on my head and she was praying for me in the middle of the store. A really deflating thing is that many people equate a serious physical limitation with mental incompetence. They see my chair and assume I'm a dumbo."

After talking with Hillam for a while, I found my imagination supplying the power to move that he didn't have. As he spoke, I began to forget that he was handicapped, that when we finished talking he wouldn't rise out of his chair, shake hands heartily and strut off. The more you talk with someone who is handicapped, I had been told, the less handicapped they appear to be.

"Last year, I paid eight thousand dollars out of my own pocket, about forty percent of my income, for medical expenses," Hillam said. "To institutionalize a quad costs twenty thousand dollars. So I'm saving taxpayers a little money, but I'd like to get ahead a bit, too. I have to pay for my wheelchair repairs. I pay Kim and Dody a hundred dollars a month each plus room and board. Together, they eat a hundred and twenty dollars' worth of food each month. All told, I figured attendant care was fifty-two hundred dollars last year. Wheelchair and equipment repair ran four hundred dollars. Catheters cost seventy-five cents each; doesn't sound like much, but I used about three hundred dollars' worth of them last year."

Hillam mentioned that auto insurance cost him a hundred dollars more than the normal rate because he uses hand controls. Lots of companies declined to insure him, even though a California study not long ago found that handicapped drivers were at least as safe as able-bodied ones. "And I had a devil of a time getting life insurance," Hillam said. "I only got it because of an influential friend. But I pay about a third more for my policy. Everybody should be responsible for some portion of his own medical care. I'm not asking for a free ride. But I think some sort of catastrophic health insurance coverage should be supplied by the government. That would cover most of the costs for somebody like me. A lot of disabled people can get jobs, but the jobs don't always provide health insurance."

Hillam paused to sip some orange juice. Since he can't move his fingers, he snatched up his glass with the heels of his hands and then lifted it to his mouth. He set it back down on the table with a clank.

"Sometimes I'll meet a girl and enjoy talking to her and

ask for a date and she absolutely won't be able to handle it," he went on. "People don't look at individuals in wheelchairs as masculine or feminine. They look at them as asexual. Well, I have the same drives as anyone else. We want to be looked upon as complete people. I dated a girl at school two years before I got my Ph.D. She told her mother she was seeing this guy who was working toward his doctorate. Her mother wrote back saying how glad she was that her daughter was finally meeting high-class types. Then the girl told her that I was in a wheelchair. Her mother started firing back letters, 'Better be careful about those types. You may have to take care of him the rest of your life. He may not be able to earn any money. What can you do together?' "

Ranking high in the large catalogue of misconceptions people have about someone confined to a wheelchair is that he's incapable of sex, and in fact has no particular longing for sex. Hillam fully intends to marry someday, when the right woman comes along, and to settle into a reasonably conventional married life. Like other quadriplegics, he has no sensitivity below his chest. However, he is capable of what's called a "reflex erection." "I can't look at the centerfold of *Playboy* and have an erection. But if I handle my penis, I can. So I can satisfy a partner during intercourse. I can't appreciate it in terms of physical release, but my partner can certainly have a climax. Sex is very much pleasing to me, and I feel the same drive toward an attractive woman as any other man. I have a story I tell when I'm asked about this. In the first James Bond movie I ever saw — it was *Goldfinger* or something — James Bond strolls into this room and goes up to the bustiest woman there. Her name, I think, is Pussy Galore. In a few minutes, she's stripped down on the bed ready for action. You know, I can't even unbutton my own shirt. So there has to be a lot of cooperation. The roles and the methods expected of each partner have to be different.

The woman has to be more active with me. But I enjoy sex. And I like seeing *Charlie's Angels* as much as anyone else."

For brunch, we drove over to some friends of Hillam's, Jake and Grayce Stipanuk. Their son, Tim, who's in his early twenties, has cerebral palsy. (This day, he was out visiting the Hearst mansion.) Grayce works as a nurse at the East San Gabriel Valley School, which ministers to severely handicapped kids. Jake used to teach school, though he recently quit to open a wheelchair repair shop. He is steadily losing his sight. The Stipanuks have long been militant members of the handicapped movement.

They used to live in Scottsdale, Arizona, a ritzy retirement community nestled outside of Phoenix, but they found themselves continually battling the schools to get their son educated. Regular classrooms didn't want him. Jake and Grayce consented, at one point, to come and sit with him in class so that he would be taught alongside able-bodied students. Among other things, he has a bad drooling problem. He has no feeling in his chin, so he doesn't know when he's drooling and when he isn't. Grayce tells him to brush his hand across his chin periodically, but he forgets. Also, he has a speech lapse. Ask him a question and you can count to three before the answer starts to come back. People encountering him for the first time think he's retarded. Scottsdale wasn't warming to the Stipanuks, so they finally came to California. "I believe Scottsdale heaved a huge sigh of relief when we rode out of town," Grayce said.

Brunch was served. Pancakes, bacon, orange juice, coffee. Hillam couldn't get his wheelchair under the table, so he sat sideways. Grayce urged everyone to have her blueberry syrup. "I think that anybody who doesn't like blueberry syrup, then they're handicapped, that's what I think," Grayce said.

"I believe I'll have a slab of bacon," Hillam interrupted. "Just stick it on there." He put out his closed hand, and Jake slapped a piece on top.

"What you need," Jake said, "is a plate with a peg coming out of the bottom. Then you can just stick the peg into your fist and have people heap food on it."

I asked Grayce about her school. "My school is good, because we don't baby the kids," she said. "Too many places don't let them do their own thing. If a kid comes to my office with a cut, I teach him to clean it and then to put a Band-Aid on. Why should I do it?"

Hillam chipped in, "People feel so goddamned self-conscious around someone in a wheelchair. You have to go out of your way to meet people. I'll be at a party and I'll say, 'Hey, did I use the wrong deodorant or something? Why's there this empty space around me?' People commonly open conversation by saying, 'Hey, is that chair electric? What's the top speed? How long does that battery last?' At least they're talking to me, but I'd like to think that I'm more than a Die-hard battery."

Jake, who is a natural raconteur and storyteller, told a favorite story of his. A friend, who is confined to a wheelchair but able to drive a hand-controlled van, wanted to see a movie. He drove over to a local theater and pulled in front of a bank to check out the billboard for the theater. Before he was able to get a good look at the times and titles, an armored car drew up beside him. He moved out of the way, circled the block, and eased up behind the armored car to get another glimpse. Nothing appealed to him, so he took off. A police car happened to spot the van circling the block and standing near the armored truck, and got immediately suspicious. It followed him. The disabled man drove onto the freeway. Two police cars were now tailing him. Four. Six. They drew him to the shoulder, leaped out of their cars, and crouched down. Shotguns were in hand. Over a bullhorn, the police ordered the man to stick his hands over his head and to climb out. He yelled that he was in a wheelchair and couldn't get out with his hands flapping in the air. A second warning thundered through the horn. Same response. The man was getting pretty worried. He imagined shotgun bullets ripping into his van and into him. At last, one of the cops snuck alongside the van and saw that the driver was indeed in a wheelchair. Six police cars full of beet-red policemen drove off.

"So you see," Jake concluded, "it can be pretty dangerous sitting in a wheelchair."

Hillam said, "I had a cop once in Los Angeles tell me to get off the street with my wheelchair. So I got onto the sidewalk. Two blocks later, another cop said I was a 'self-propelled vehicle' and had to move onto the street."

Jake said, "Some of these people don't realize that they could be in a wheelchair tomorrow. That would shake up their attitudes."

I asked Grayce whether Tim's attitude about himself had improved because of the way they brought him up.

"My God, yes," she answered. "He was very, very maladjusted as a child. He was extremely conscious of his disability. He couldn't accept his drooling. I even had a hypnotist try to cure him, with no luck. I remember when he was about fourteen, I took him to the county fair, thinking that would cheer him up. I said I'd buy him some ice cream. He loved ice cream. He said no, someone would see him and laugh. Now, he's maybe too confident. Like he'll do a wheelie for you on the front lawn if you ask him. I've worked hard to make him independent. Any time he wants something, I say, 'Hey, Tim, are you crippled or something that you can't do it yourself?' I confess that I didn't do that when he was younger. We've learned, also."

The matter of legislation came up. Everyone agreed that plenty of laws had been put on the books that barred discrimination against the handicapped. The trouble was getting those laws enforced.

Hillam said, "A law passed in California said that any new public buildings over ten thousand square feet must be totally accessible to wheelchairs. So we're seeing a lot of buildings going up that are nine thousand nine hundred and ninety square feet."

Jake said, "In La Verne, an ordinance has been passed that reserves parking spaces for the handicapped. They're marked by blue paint, but the mayor has said that he has no money for blue paint. So La Verne has no blue curbs."

"La Verne is a funny town," Grayce said. "It's got to be educated. And we're here to educate it. We want this to be a town for everybody."

An airplane whooshed overhead. We all looked up.

"One thing for sure," Grayce said. "If a person has to be disabled, if some child has to come into this world disabled, I'd much rather he be disabled right now than twenty-three years ago, when Tim was born. It's a very exciting time for the disabled. There's so much going on."

We talked around the dining table for hours beyond brunch. By now, the pancakes were well digested, and we were talked out. Hillam and I took our leave. The sun was strong. The temperature had crept well into the eighties.

When we arrived back at Hillam's house, we sat out on the patio and relaxed. The lawn was wild with grass. The boy who cut Hillam's lawn was on vacation.

I wondered whether Hillam suffered many medical ailments.

"Every now and then I have quad pain," he said. "That's phantom pain. We all have this. With me, my feet feel tingly and hot. You just ignore it as best you can. Some quads, though, have it so bad they have surgery done. I'm also very susceptible to bladder infections, since I don't have control of my bowels and bladder. And I'm sensitive to heat. I don't realize I'm getting too much sun until I turn into a beet."

A harried-looking Dody came out and said a call had come for Hillam. Excusing himself, he slipped his wheelchair into gear, spun around and rolled inside. While he was gone, Dody told me a little about her job.

"I had never had any experience with a handicapped person before," she said. "I suppose I was a little afraid of them. But I needed some money and when I saw Bruce's ad, I figured why not? I liked him immediately. Caring for him has been a pleasure. He had a hard time getting any attendants for a while. One of those who applied, he told me, wondered if he minded if the guy carried a gun. Bruce is terrific because he doesn't allow any time for sorrow. By now, I don't really think of him as being handicapped. Gotta tell you, this has turned out to be one neat job."

She took a breath and went on, "Ideally, Bruce wants his attendants to become his friends, not simply his employees. He's told me that he thinks of the relationship as a sort of brother-sister one. The attendant, I feel, becomes an extension of the family. In some respects, though, you have to put the person you're caring for ahead of yourself. You can't just dash out the door whenever you feel like it. You can't say you'll be home at a certain hour and then arrive much later. Bruce told me that a friend of his characterized the relationship as having, for the attendant, all of the disadvantages of marriage with none of the advantages. There're some grains of truth in that, all right."

Hillam returned, smiling, and Dody went back into the house to do some vacuuming, humming a tune to herself as she moved across the floors. Hillam sat languidly, with his arms resting on his knees and his hands beneath his chin. Every so often, he would swing his arms back so one was slung over the arm of his chair and the other reposed on top of his head. He was quiet for a bit. I asked him if he was ever bitter about his handicap.

He pondered that for just a moment. Then he said, "You always think about what it would have been like if you weren't handicapped. I don't look back on September 9, 1961, as one of my luckier days. Initially, I wondered a lot about the justice of it all. But ever since college, I've kept up a positive attitude. I do wonder how I might have been different. Since my father was in the service for twenty years, I probably would have joined the service. I probably would be an engineer, and I might now be looking to start my own company. Be my own man. I probably would do a lot of backpacking. As far as people I associate with, I don't think that would be so much different. There's a girl I see now and then who plays tennis. I'd love to play with her, though it doesn't bother me that she plays instead with other people. I think my life is as complete as anyone else's. Life to me is very worth living. I can't see any reason at all for resenting that I'm alive. People have come up to me and said that if they were me they'd commit suicide. I just smile. I'm in love with life."

2

Had clumps of handicapped people settled the colonies, most disabled people believe, America today would be totally accessible to the handicapped. But that isn't the way it happened, and the halt and lame have been mired in obscurity for two hundred years. They have been locked away in institutions, crowded into attics, shuttled into basements. They became the hidden minority, their plight stored painfully in their heads and shared only with equally disabled individuals. Since the hale and hearty neither expected nor required the handicapped to work, architecture and attitudes developed with the sound in mind. All of this left a stigma that has never worn off. The handicapped were in a different line of business than the able-bodied. They couldn't get into or out of most buildings. They couldn't ride the subway, hop onto buses, fly in planes. They couldn't grab hold of pay phones. They couldn't squeeze into public restrooms. Many were banished from schools, and most found it difficult or impossible to get jobs. More than this, they were having problems with their own psyches, their marriages, abuse, the law.

The handicapped were a different minority in more ways than one. They boasted members from every race and re-

ligion, both sexes and all ages. And, as handicapped groups
like to point out, membership can be conferred on anyone
at any time. It doesn't take much. A skiing accident. A slip
in the bathtub. A wrenching tackle on the football field. A
wrong dose of medicine. A car skidding out of control. Disability can take seconds, or years. After all, most disabled
people were once able-bodied. Only about one in every six
was born disabled. The handicapped have gotten into the
habit of referring to anyone who isn't disabled as a TAB,
or Temporarily Able-Bodied. "Not anyone can become a
black or a woman," one movement leader told me. "But
anyone can become handicapped. You could, tomorrow."

Strangely enough, World War II — which, like every war,
swelled the size of the disabled population — had much to
do with hatching the handicapped-rights movement. After
throngs of America's workers had been trucked off to war,
employers had to hire whatever was left. Many of the
workers remaining were crippled. The Ford Motor Company alone snapped up eleven thousand handicapped employees, and, all told, more than eighty percent of the country's industries added disabled workers. To the surprise of
many people, most handicapped employees showed that they
were worth their hire. Industries gleefully reported smaller
labor turnover, lower absenteeism, fewer accidents, and pro-
duction rates that equaled or exceeded previous norms.

Once the shooting stopped, however, returning veterans
began to push handicapped workers out of the job market
and back into their attics and basements. They bristled at
this. They felt they were being sold down the river. They
had gotten their taste of being part of society, and they liked
it. They realized that social upheaval was necessary. The
pressing problem, though, was putting food on the table. So,
at first, the handicapped set about trying to get themselves
educated so that they could find work. Their voices were

quiet. Not till the 1960s were the first real rumblings of mobilization heard. The deaf, the blind, and cerebral palsy victims were the first to organize. "What do we do?" they asked each other. "We are being stopped by six-inch curbs. Doors must be at least thirty inches wide for wheelchairs to pass through; almost all of this country's doors are narrower than twenty-four inches. The blind can't 'read' printed signs unless the letters are raised. The deaf can't 'hear' spoken announcements unless lights or printed instructions accompany them. Elevator buttons are just too high for people in wheelchairs." What was the proper response? Scream bloody murder? It was pretty hard to know. Many people were frightened of the handicapped; if the body was twisted, they reasoned, so was the mind. The handicapped had almost no credibility. Worse, the movement was hopelessly factionalized. Other minorities were far better organized. Being disabled didn't help. Many of the handicapped couldn't walk. Others couldn't talk. Or hear. Or see. Their pockets were empty.

As the years dragged on, however, the situation became a lot harder to ignore. The already gigantic number of handicapped people continued to grow. Medical science had begun to work its magic. It slew some diseases and stalled others. People were surviving the ailments and accidents of early and middle age and living to a point hitherto unknown except in biblical lore. In 1900, the average life expectancy was forty-seven years; by the 1970s it had stretched to seventy-one. By the year 2000, the disabled population will parallel the number of able-bodied persons. The annual U.S. mortality rate for spinal-cord cases, for example, tumbled from ninety percent at the close of World War I to below fifteen percent after World War II. In the 1920s, victims of Down's syndrome were lucky to make it beyond their teens; now they often live happily into their forties. What's more, an influx of some 490,000 disabled soldiers came home from Vietnam; faced with widespread unemployment, treated as villains rather than as heroes, they snapped and snarled. They had a lot to grumble about. No federal legislation specifically barred discrimination against the handicapped. State laws that protected them were hopelessly weak and appropriations for enforcement were ridiculously inadequate. And so several hundred groups representing a medley of disabilities began to agitate for laws that would guard their rights. They arranged public hearings, they spoke at meetings, they presented position papers, they cultivated the press, and they got front-page publicity.

The crux of the crisis was pretty obvious – a handicap, whatever its nature, does not automatically deny fame, fortune, or fulfillment. And why should it? Plato and Poe were hunchbacks. Milton and Homer were blind. Handel was lame. Shelley and Spinoza were cripples. Beethoven doubtlessly never heard his final heroic symphonies, as deafness closed in on him. Edison couldn't hear. Van Gogh was an epileptic. So was Caesar. Franklin Roosevelt was a four-term president in a wheelchair. Helen Keller surmounted the triple handicaps of blindness, deafness, and consequently the inability to speak. The electrical genius Steinmetz and the great French writer Voltaire conquered mutilated bodies to go on to benefit all of mankind. So the handicapped argued that instead of being looked on as perpetual children – helpless and hopeless – they, too, wanted to become part of the rest of society and be helped to lead lives as close to normal as possible.

As the handicapped-rights movement gathered steam, men like paraplegic Ron Kovic, a Vietnam vet and author of the eloquent and moving *Born on the Fourth of July*, became vehement spokesmen for the disabled. In May 1970, a clutch of handicapped New Yorkers, spearheaded by an angry young woman rejected for a teaching post, formed Disabled in Action, probably the movement's first truly militant organization ("We're the ones who make the trouble," is how one charter member explained the group). Waving placards and chanting rallying cries ("You gave us your dimes. Now allow us our dignity"), the handicapped became a force to be reckoned with. They howled their upset.

"We have been denied our rights. We want them. And we're not going to shut up until we get them."

"Somebody can be put down and walked over only so long before he fights back. We've been the doormats of society for as long as we're going to be."

"All we want is our day in the sun."

"Everybody seems shocked by what we want. Why is it so shocking? What's so shocking about wanting to get around and have a social life? What's so shocking about wanting to hold a job and earn one's keep? What's so shocking about wanting to see more of the world than what shows up through a hospital window?"

"People don't want us to darken their doors. They treat us like the bubonic plague."

"Don't we mean anything? Don't we matter to anyone?"

"We're not attractions in the zoo. I'm not a rhesus monkey. My wife's not a water buffalo."

"We have a terrible past with which to live, and we don't want to wrap it in sentimental ribbons. We don't want dewy-eyed pity. We want our rights."

"The able-bodied hold all the cards. We feel it's high time we got dealt a hand."

"Either deal us a hand or stop the game."

"Not only deal us a hand, deal us a few aces."

"In the 1960s, a political and legal revolution began because there was a significant minority population that had to sit at the back of the bus. Today there is a significant minority that cannot even get on the bus."

"Society would like to wish out of existence the whole population of disfigured people. Wishing won't make us go away, just as wishing won't make us look better."

"They embarrass us until we want to slip through cracks in the floor."

"We live by encouragement, and without it we die. Slowly, protractedly, sadly, and angrily."

"It is considered one of the traditional, hospitable, democratic imperatives that some less fortunates will always be carried on society's back, and of course it sounds admirable. But, unfortunately, when help is forced unnecessarily down unwilling throats (and mine was a throat they tried to pry open) through impoverished legislation, that is no longer a rather kind charity. That is a disgrace."

Things began to happen. Steadily, individual states began to yield domino-fashion to the handicapped ground swell, enacting a wash of laws that forbade discrimination. Still, nothing much was happening on the federal level. The movement went into a phase of getting nowhere — the long meetings into the dead of night, thermos coffee, the gradual breaking of the glaze that comes with getting up at 3 A.M. The protests. The calls to congressmen, nice replies, no action. Yawns. Plans for tomorrow. Go home. Nothing much accomplished. Were they talking to the moon?

By 1972, a vast Rehabilitation Act had stumbled through Congress, only to be stopped twice in its tracks by Richard Nixon. "Too costly," was his basic explanation. The handicapped felt they had gotten a royal rooking. In May 1973, a widely publicized protest march was staged by people in wheelchairs organized by Disabled in Action. Some one hundred and fifty sallow-faced handicapped agitators, including a paralyzed mother with a baby cuddled in her arms, were moved by sympathizers, a number of whom were themselves deaf or otherwise disabled, from the Lincoln Memorial to Capitol Hill. Threading their way through thick mid-morning traffic with a police escort, the protestors clacked along the two-and-a-half-mile route for almost three hours. It was a stirring sight, the kind that makes the chest swell. Onlookers lining the streets dabbed at their eyes with handkerchiefs. The sight of misshapen people out and shouting for help was a potent one.

At long last, in September 1973, Congress passed and President Nixon signed a scaled-down Rehabilitation Act for the physically and mentally limited, a mighty ziggurat of legislation comparable in its implications to the Civil Rights Act of 1968. "No otherwise qualified handicapped individual shall, solely by the reason of his handicap, be excluded from participation in, be denied the benefits of, or otherwise be subjected to discrimination under any program or activity receiving federal financial assistance," it declared. Also it set up a board to govern the Architectural Barriers Act of 1968, an ambitious measure that required public facilities built after 1968 with federal dollars to be accessible to the disabled. It had been passed but was ignored because no enforcement procedures had been established. Long after the publicity had receded, the social and political effects of the Rehabilitation Act would still be poignantly felt. Everyone would be affected by it. In elemental respects, the character of the country would eventually change.

Celebration was not totally in order. Though legislation now existed, nothing much happened for a time. As the years went by, bureaucrats thrashed about trying to figure out how to word the rules of compliance. Barring discrimination was fine, but what were the rules? What constituted discrimination, and what didn't? What concessions had to be made? The handicapped dug in their heels. Get those rules out or else, they said. Still, their organization was wanting. The movement was an act of faith, but it was also a thousand small movements, each rowing vigorously in its own direction. In 1974, a hundred and fifty disabled persons got together in Washington, D.C., and formed the American Coalition of Citizens with Disabilities to oversee the multifarious activities of all handicapped people. The coalition galvanized the handicapped community and salved its need for a sense of direction. A hopeful sign appeared. The next year, the Education for All Handicapped Children Act cleared Congress, assuring all disabled children of the right to a free public education. One educator summed it up best. "It overcomes," he said, "two hundred years of sin."

Progress stalled during the Ford-Carter transition. Regulations had been drafted by the Ford people, but now Carter's men wished to study them before putting anything into effect. Morale in the handicapped world slumped. Telephone wires from coast to coast pulsated with pleas and threats, imprecations and exculpations. In San Francisco, over a hundred people lugged mattresses, food, and battery chargers for their motorized wheelchairs into the regional Health, Education and Welfare office. They hung around for twenty-five days. "We were prepared to stay forever," one occupier declared. In Washington, demonstrators tottered after HEW Secretary Joseph Califano from his office to his home, to his public appearances, back to his office and back home, clucking their tongues. These people are in a bad way, they told him. Do something!

Responding to the sympathy the sit-ins roused, Califano speeded up his schedule and, in April 1977, at last signed regulations making the key portions of the Rehabilitation Act effective (other federal agencies are still drafting their own rules). The handicapped breathed a sigh of relief. The thunder receded.

"A great day. Things better start happening now."

"The time will never come when I can throw my wheelchair away. But the time might now come when it won't hold me back."

"Today, it seems, the handicapped at last become people."

Califano said, "The act opens up a new era of civil rights in America, and will work fundamental changes in many facets of American life. It reflects the recognition of the Congress that most handicapped persons can lead proud and productive lives, despite their disabilities. It will usher in a new era of equality for handicapped individuals in which unfair barriers to self-sufficiency and decent treatment will begin to fall before the force of the law."

The general drift of the regulations was this. Employers doing work with the government may not refuse to hire the handicapped — including cancer and heart disease sufferers — if their handicaps don't interfere with their ability to do the job. That meant a major overhaul in the administering of pre-employment physical examinations. An offer of employment could be conditioned on the successful completion of a medical exam, as long as the offer wasn't withdrawn on the basis of a medical condition that wasn't job related, a provision particularly helpful to people stricken by cancer. Fringe benefits could be modified or withdrawn only if the insurer could prove an actuarial basis for doing so. Furthermore, employers had to make "reasonable accommodations" for their handicapped workers. And they had to launch aggressive affirmative action plans so that handicapped people are sought out, hired, and promoted.

The rules specified that all new buildings be made accessible to the disabled through ramps, elevators, and other appurtenances; many existing buildings would also have to be modified. Within sixty days all school programs not requiring structural changes had to be made available to the handicapped. A political science class, for instance, that was situated high in a building without an elevator had to be moved to a ground floor or to another building that had elevators. Programs needing physical alterations, such as a science lab, had three years to comply. The new regulations meant, in part, that every school, college, social service center, hospital, or clinic built after June 1, 1977, the effective date of the regulations, had to be entirely usable by handicapped people, including those in wheelchairs. Hospitals had to work out special methods for treating the disabled (such as a way to communicate with the deaf in emergency rooms). Physicians who treated Medicaid or Medicare patients, or whose offices were in a hospital or clinic built with federal dollars, had to make their offices accessible to the handicapped, or to come up with an arrangement to treat them, even if that meant making house calls. All public school programs enabling the handicapped to be mainstreamed had to be ready by September 1978.

A thorny problem arose at once: What to do with the country's ten million alcoholics, and its million and a half drug addicts? Does a person hooked on the bottle or the needle deserve a job? The federal government's answer: Protect them as well. Employers, however, needn't hire them if they had miserable work records. The range and vagueness of parts of the regulations, which allow exceptions based on "undue hardship," were expected to be the basis of litigation for years. They would be mighty costly, too. All in all, HEW officials concluded, implementing the legislation would require more than $2.4 billion a year. Not all of that would be new money; some of the amount is already being spent under other laws. The government also hoped that the cost would be balanced out with the productivity of newly employed handicapped people. In enforcing the guidelines, Califano stressed that HEW would be "guided by sensitivity, fairness and common sense."

No one really knows how many handicapped people are out there in need of protection. The numbers flutter all over the lot. Some estimates range giddily up to seventy million. The 1970 U.S. Census, the first to ask about disabilities, came up with a figure of forty million, but that didn't include handicapped in institutions or the numberless people thought to have omitted mention of their disabilities, for whatever the reason. The National Arts and the Handicapped Information Service calculated that some fifty million persons are handicapped, in roughly the following proportions (some people fall into several categories): 11.7 million people physically disabled (including half a million people in wheelchairs and three million who depend on crutches, canes, braces, or walkers); 12.5 million temporarily injured (broken limb, back injury, severe burns); 2.4 million deaf; 11 million with impaired hearing; 1.3 million blind; 8.2 million visually handicapped; 6.8 million mentally disabled; 1.7 million homebound (chronic health disorders, wasting diseases); 2.1 million institutionalized (mentally disturbed, mentally retarded, terminal illness).

I dwell on these gloomy statistics only because of the odd disproportion between the number of disabled people in this country and the number most people commonly assume. This imbalance exists, of course, because of the invisibility of the handicapped population. You can stroll, as I have, from Lower Manhattan to Central Park and back and not see a wheelchair, although, if your eye is reasonably alert, you would doubtless spot thousands of people.

With the spread of the movement, the disabled have slowly begun to shed some of their invisibility, and, in fact, have become something of a popular feature of contemporary life. In May 1977 they were the focus of a White House Conference on the Handicapped. Washington's Sheraton-Park Hotel, the site of the meeting, ordered seventy-five thousand dollars' worth of permanent renovations to accommodate the unusual delegates. Half of the twenty-five hundred state delegates and participants were disabled. The hotel replaced some bathroom doors, shortened the legs of vanities, lowered the phones in telephone booths, whipped up menus in braille. Superficial and poorly organized, the conference achieved little of substance, but a good many people were exposed to disability for the first time. Among the lofty figures to drop in was President Carter himself, who trumpeted, "The time for discrimination against the handicapped in America is over."

The movement has spawned a children's newspaper cartoon strip called "Wee Pals," which follows the antics of disabled people. Hollywood has begun to discover the handicapped. A movie, *The Other Side of the Mountain,* chronicling the life of a skier who becomes paralyzed, has been applauded by the handicapped, as has *Coming Home,* which portrays a romance between a paraplegic war veteran and an able-bodied woman. Two giant brokerage firms — Shearson, Hayden Stone and E. F. Hutton — have installed teletypewriters in their offices so they can service deaf investors. (Shearson immediately picked up a client who poured fifty thousand dollars into the market.) A Phoenix department store has hired salespeople proficient in sign language. A $2.4 million recreation center for the handicapped has gone up in Washington, D.C., and the Lincoln Memorial has been outfitted with both an elevator and a ramp. The Omaha telephone directory routinely runs a listing of accessible buildings and businesses (Hinky Dinky Stores, Ace Hardware, Dundee Barber, Chu's Chop Suey). The *Advocate,* the nation's biggest gay paper, recently included an article on gays who are handicapped. Two glossy pages in an issue of *Glamour* magazine set forth the latest tips in wheelchair fashions ("Pullovers or loose cowlnecks are easy to get on and much neater-looking than cardigans which tend to bunch up when sitting." "Watch out for clothes with back seaming, pockets or zippers. They can be a problem. Even if you have no pain sensation, they can cause skin irritations." "Pay more attention to your hands and neck — that's where people's attention tends to focus. Polish on nails, if not too dark, can be attractive."). Several parking spots at Bloomingdale's in Paramus, New Jersey, and King Kullen in Bridgehampton, Long Island, and at shopping malls across the nation are set aside for the disabled. Lily Tomlin saw fit to come up with a marvelously witty skit in which she plays Crystal the Quadriplegic, a tough-talking lady who has a CB radio mounted on her wheelchair, which she uses to chatter with truckers. She is fond of hitchhiking and her heartfelt ambition is to hang-glide in her chair off the Pacific Palisades. "Walkies gotta worry about crashing and hurting themselves," she says. "I'm just out for a good time."

Fine. But what things really boiled down to were whether anything was going to be different now. Would the euphoria and enthusiasm generated by the legislation be sustained and translated into tangible gains for the many millions who live with disabilities? How long would it take? The law hasn't really been tested yet and it is still malleable. Handicapped groups wince at the absurdities that still persist. Disabled foreigners are barred from immigrating into the United States, with rare exceptions. At least seventeen states have statutes outlawing marriage by people who have epilepsy; more than double that number disallow marriages between the mentally retarded. Only recently did Chicago repeal an "ugly law," a variation of which remains in force in Columbus and Omaha. The Chicago statute said that no one "diseased, maimed, mutilated or in any way deformed so as to be an unsightly or disgusting object" may step out in public.

The Coalition of Citizens with Disabilities, which speaks for fifty-five groups and seven million disabled people, thinks the major task for the handicapped is making sure the legislation is translated into action. The coalition's director, Frank Bowe, a psychologist deaf from a bout with measles at the age of three, told me, "The legislation is there. It exists. We await its enforcement, and we will monitor it closely." People regularly phone the coalition and find themselves speaking to Bowe. How is that possible? He has an assistant on an extension, who passes on to Bowe in sign language what is being said. Bowe is so good at the system that you'd never guess he wasn't listening himself.

"One thing a lot of people neglect to think about," Bowe said, "is that these rules apply to federally funded programs. The private sector is another matter. Some buildings are being built without government dollars. Some employers don't get any money from Uncle Sam. We must work on that, as well. The struggle will be a long one, and no one doubts it will be a hard one. We are overcoming many, many years of disgrace. And remember, we are talking about changes that will, sooner or later, affect everyone. The hardest thing of all may well be to get others to see us as people, not as crutches and wheelchairs and canes."

Much remains to be found out about the handicapped minority. Laws and legislators tell only part of the story. Some of their problems beggar description. The sense of being unwanted has been imposed upon them for so long, it has found every conceivable form. Much of their story lies far away from Capitol Hill, in both strange and ordinary places, in grammar schools and colleges, in pleasant-looking houses and apartments on shady streets in small towns.

3

A DARK-HAIRED, soft-featured woman in her early thirties, nervy in manner, Virginia Granato lives on the outskirts of New York. I looked her up one cool afternoon, and she produced cans of soda, ice, and glasses, drew her motorized wheelchair up to the dining table, and talked with me for hours. She lives in a box of an apartment in an ordinary-looking high-rise on an ordinary block of similar apartment houses. The space was limited, but she had arranged her furniture adeptly, so that I didn't feel nudged or threatened. The walls were that general color that can be called beige or oatmeal, and hanging on the longest wall, above a sofa thronged with multifoam cushions, was a print of a rural scene. Across the room on a wall shelf stood a shiny bowling trophy. It belonged to her uncle, who had left it there as a subtle joke.

Without any small talk, beyond asking me whether I found the temperature cool or not cool enough (it was exactly right), Virginia plunged straight into her story. "I want the truth known," she said, sitting upright. "I believe everyone should know about our difficulties. I will speak out whenever I can. Handicapped folks haven't had a say in this country. We haven't had a shred of power. You can be mighty sure that what the handicapped need is last on a lot of people's list, and it's not moving up all that fast. Discrimination has been one of the givens in our lives, and none of us like it. It's going to take a lot to polish our image, but it must be done. We are not evil. Mainstreaming the handicapped is more than a political or legal decision, it's more than anything you read about in the papers. It's people's lives."

When I asked her some biographical questions, Virginia sat straight and prim as a furled umbrella, and said that she was born and reared in Queens. Her father was a factory laborer, and now works as a pattern cutter in a dusty loft in Manhattan's garment district. She said she had been a "very, very active child," and even as she sat in her living room with me, she emanated restlessness. "I sang, I danced, I played sports," she said. "I rode my bike. I was a real tomboy. Oh, how I loved to dance. How I loved to sing. I probably would have pursued an entertainment career had the dice fallen differently."

It began with a headache. An awful headache. This was 1955. Virginia was nine. Day by day, the headache got steadily worse. Next, a stiff neck. Trouble breathing. Gradual weakness. Nausea. Her parents decided she should go to the hospital. These were the final days of the big epidemic of polio that raced across the East Coast, leaving paralysis in its wake. However, the Salk vaccine was out in the field and being administered at schools. They were giving it out by age, youngest first. Virginia was in the fourth grade. "That week I felt the headache, I was scheduled to get the vaccine. I got polio instead."

The day after she entered the hospital, she was packed into an iron lung. While a freshly scrubbed nurse stood next to her attempting to explain something about how the lung worked, a priest delivered the last rites. A deep confusion possessed her. "I was just a child, so what did I know? It was a chilling experience. My heart would beat fast as if I had been racing. I just wanted to get better and get the hell out of there. It's an experience I wouldn't want to wish on anyone. I'd much rather wish death." For a month, she was kept in the lung. When she was removed, paralysis extended from her neck on down. The only movements she could make were facial expressions, and she made as many different faces as she could out of fear that she would soon lose that power as well. Soon after, she was taken to a state rehabilitation hospital in northern New York, and for the next fourteen months she endured a grueling physical routine to try to recapture some movement.

Strength began to return in many muscles of her arms. She learned to feed herself, to dress herself partially, to cope with the unending depression. "It was torture," she said. "My attitude was, 'Why me? Why in God's name me?' I was bitter. Very bitter. Mostly against my parents. I don't know why. I guess I had to blame someone, and they were convenient. Brother, was I a miserable pill to them. I'd yell at them, make them feel it was their fault, twist and twist the guilt into them."

Upon discharge from the hospital, she returned to Queens. Refusing to hire an attendant, her mother insisted on caring for her alone. For some time, however, her mother and father hadn't been getting along, and the introduction of a handicapped child into the household didn't help matters. They stopped going places. Friends were rarely invited over. The family included an older brother, and soon after Virginia came home a sister was born. "It was clear that I was a burden to everyone." When Virginia turned sixteen, she came down with a bad cold and had to be hospitalized in Goldwater Hospital. "I realized I had things there I didn't have at home. Handicapped kids my own age. People to play games with. At home, I was not much more than a plant, a piece of fruit. It was difficult to meet people when you were in a wheelchair. All the girls my age were dating already. I wasn't. So one day when my cold was cured, I asked the doctor if I could stay at the hospital. He agreed, and so I did."

Just as she had hoped, the hospital proved to be good for Virginia. In short order, she met a network of people she liked. There were movies and shows to see. Periodic day trips to Manhattan were organized. She struck up a friendship there with another girl her age, also a polio victim. The girl's brother lived in a foster home in Manhattan, and he would visit on weekends. Frequently he brought along a friend, George Shorter (not his real name), another resident at the home, who had been an orphan virtually all of his life. Almost immediately, George took an interest in Virginia, and she in him. This was 1965. George was seventeen, Virginia nineteen.

"We just thoroughly enjoyed each other's company," Virginia said. "He had nobody else. I didn't have much else. Things began to perk up. I didn't have a motorized chair at the time, so he would take me outdoors and push me around. He seemed to get a kick out of steering me, though I'd complain he was a lousy driver. It was beautiful on the grounds of the hospital in the summer. Lovely trees. The water in the distance. Birds wheeling overhead. The quiet. We listened to records a lot together. We both liked records. I was feeling very grateful. Life had begun to recede into another cube of time-and-space. I thought many times I was watching a movie, it seemed too good to be true."

She stopped for a moment and pushed herself back from the table, daydreaming, I supposed. She sipped some Coke, then returned close to me.

Fed up with a lifetime of living in foster homes, George one day decided to volunteer for the Army. He served two years in Vietnam, writing faithfully to Virginia. When he got back to the States, he told her he wanted to marry her. "My immediate reaction was, 'No way. Forget it.' The whole idea seemed idiotic. Not long before, I had been thinking of becoming a nun. When I did some checking into it, however, I discovered that no order would take a handicapped person. That always struck me as pretty ludicrous. But when you're handicapped, many doors are closed to you. I knew, though, that if I got married he would tire of me. Quite frankly, it would be an ordeal having me as a wife. It would be too damned much of a strain."

She debated it for days, and at length her resistance dwindled and caved in. "I was probably influenced somewhat by my situation at the time. Here I was living in a hospital, surrounded by other disabled people. We got along just fine. We didn't have bad attitudes about each other. I had forgotten what it was like out there. I was no longer in touch with the discrimination against us." They were engaged on Valentine's Day of 1970.

In due course, they set out one afternoon to buy an engagement ring. The jeweler they picked had his shop in a loft building, and when they arrived there, the elevator operator refused to take them up. "We don't take wheelchairs," he told them. Angry and uneasy, they called the manager, and the operator finally took them up when no one else was in the car. "Here I was with my future husband and I knew this was his first taste of what it was going to be like. It wasn't going to get any better than this. I was being reminded of how society regarded the handicapped — these fearsome, frightening, grotesque people who must have per-petual hospital care. There is a special mixture of fear and fascination and hatred. We would be out in public sometimes and I would hear people whispering, 'Oh how sad. I wonder what happened to her.'"

The marriage took place on a hot and splendidly sunny day in a cathedral on East 68th Street in Manhattan. It started out as a fairly small affair, but the guest list grew. All of Virginia's friends from Goldwater crowded into the church, giving it the vague look of a hospital ward. The *Daily News* dispatched a reporter and photographer to cover the event. For the most part, Virginia remembers it as a euphoric occasion. "But I also knew there were all these people, lots and lots of people, just waiting to tell me, 'I told you so.'"

They settled down in a shabby but adequate apartment in a Queens project. George had found a job driving a cab, then switched to a position in the post office. While in Gold-water, Virginia had taken a series of secretarial courses, and she managed to get a secretarial job at the hospital. They installed themselves in the life of newlyweds. Since they both worked, they weren't entitled to public assistance, and couldn't afford an attendant. For a year, George took care of Virginia's needs, getting up extra early to dress her in the morning. Then it began to prove too difficult, and a nursing student was found to roll Virginia out of bed.

"Was it a good marriage?" I asked.

"No, I suppose not," she said.

"Because of your being handicapped?"

"Right."

"He tired of it?"

"You've got it."

He was tall, abrupt, quiet. He wasn't much of a socializer. "He loved me in a funny sort of way, I believe, but I felt he was ashamed to be seen in public with me. He realized by now how people reacted to somebody seen with a handicapped person."

After a time, he quit his postal job and started driving a truck. Preferring long hauls, he would sometimes be away for days. An attendant had to be brought in to care for Virginia. The marriage disintegrated. Everything was grist for argument. Eventually, Virginia filed for divorce. She neither saw nor heard from her husband. He agreed to whatever her lawyer asked. "Boy, was I scared. I had no idea if I could hack it, if I could make it on my own."

Day after day, she swallowed one, two, three green-and-aqua tranquilizers as soon as she woke. This helped a little. She went in for psychotherapy. "I would go off to my bedroom, close the door and sit before the mirror and practice a speech to myself to give me courage. 'Must stay calm and collected,' I kept repeating. 'People will accept you better when you're calm and collected.' "

Virginia sipped some Coke. She slapped the glass down, and the liquid swirled across the table, wetting some books. She reached for a paper napkin to sop the soda.

"I couldn't get it out of my mind that it would have resolved some things had I been walking," she said. "Had I been more independent, I think the marriage might have worked. But I'm not an idealist. I'm a realist. I don't regret the marriage. I learned a lot from it."

In early 1977, she moved. She knew she had to. For one thing, the one elevator where she lived broke down repeatedly, leaving her cocooned in her apartment. Half the time she missed work. She had no friends in the immediate area. The move changed her. Newly divorced, she felt virginal again, years younger. Beginning anew.

I heard a clatter in the bedroom, and a wiry boy in his late teens who looked after Virginia on the weekends padded into the room. A tuft of hair stood up on the back of his head. Shyly, he asked if either of us cared for anything to eat or drink. We said we didn't. Shrugging his shoulders, he shuffled over to the couch, plumped up some pillows and plopped down. He began to munch on some saltines, then he picked up a piece of paper from the coffee table and started to doodle on it.

"This person takes real good care of me," Virginia said. "He doesn't regard me as some piece of luggage, now do you?"

The boy looked up. "Nah, only when you yell at me," he said.

"I only yell at you," she cut in, "when you get lazy and think that I can do more for myself than I can."

After she moved, Virginia energetically undertook to acquire friends, and before long she had an enviable reputation for certain of her skills, notably her way in the kitchen. "There's one thing I can really do," she said, "and that's cook up a storm. I am handy at the stove." She has become social and gregarious. She is known for her chatty way, her fondness for telling stories. Neighbors throng to her apartment like seagulls around a piling. "Beforehand, I hardly had any contact with people. Phone calls now and then, that was about it. I never felt I could get out. I wanted to see some action. I missed that. I was in many ways unhappy. Here, I have some pretty good friends. Some people, I know, are still scared of me, don't want to have anything to do with me, but you face that everywhere. I doubt I'll live to see that wiped out entirely." Sure that her battery is charged up, Virginia with fair regularity makes the circuit from apartment to apartment in her building, looking in on neighbors, passing the latest gossip. Friends figure she has had it as hard as someone can have it, so they turn to her as sage and mentor. She can swell a room with her talk.

One of her neighbors had told me, "When I first got to

know her, I was a bit uneasy about her condition. I didn't know how to behave. What possibly did we have in common? I kept asking myself. I suppose I often made a total fool of myself. Now I don't see the wheelchair. Not everyone here is like that, unfortunately. It's a dirty shame the way some people are."

I asked Virginia if she is still bitter about being handicapped.

"Yeah, sure I am," she answered. "I just don't understand the discrimination. I guess it all boils down to America playing up the body. Looking beautiful. Beautiful bodies. If you don't look like Tom Terrific or Barbara Body, you're an outcast. It's sort of like we're all carbon copies. All the black guys have a certain look, all the white girls have a certain look, all the white guys have a certain look. If you look different or act different, you should be shunned. We've got to say to people, 'Hey, here we are. We're not like everybody else. We're here, though. Whether you like it or not, we're here. You're going to have to learn to live with us.'"

Would she marry again? I asked.

Her answer was immediate. "No. Absolutely not," she said. "I will never subject myself to that pain again. I'm looking for a married man who wants to have an affair. Relationships today don't last in general. For a marriage with a handicapped person to last, it would take an exceptional person. There aren't too many exceptional people floating around. Remember, I'm a realist. I don't live in Never-Never Land."

She continued, "I think the chances are awfully slight that a nonhandicapped and a handicapped person can marry and have a successful marriage. I've had some friends who have tried it also, and it didn't work. Attitudes are the problem more than the physical thing. Some day, I would hope, such marriages will be common. But I probably won't be around.

I mean, when you go out looking for someone, you don't say to yourself, 'Well, I think I'll look for a girl in a wheelchair tonight.' For me, once was enough. I'm not like the movie *Once Is Not Enough.*"

"You mean, you're not going to marry me," the boy on the sofa chipped in.

Virginia threw her head back and laughed.

"Haven't I made my distinct lack of interest in you clear yet?" she said.

"Can't a guy hope?"

It had become late. Virginia, as usual, was expecting some company later, and so I got ready to go. She started her chair, spun it around in a circle, and escorted me to the door the same as any gracious hostess would.

She fell silent and pensive for a moment, then added one final thought. "It's funny that in my dreams I'm never handicapped. This is common with people who aren't born handicapped. I see myself walking around like everybody else. But just a couple of weeks ago, for the first time, I remember waking up and recalling a dream of myself in a wheelchair. It was something that actually happened to me as a child. I was being carried up the steps of a church to go to mass. The point is, even if other people haven't accepted me as completely as I'd like, my subconscious, after all these years, seems to be finally accepting my handicap."

4

DOES a place exist where the handicapped are totally welcome? I was told things were different in Berkeley, California. They make revolutions in Berkeley. This is where the Free Speech and the People's Park struggles found their momentum. The hotbed of liberal fervor. In more recent years, something new and positive was happening here. The handicapped were clanking into town and living independent lives. The reason for all the action, I was told almost reverently, was the Center for Independent Living.

The center crouched low on Telegraph Avenue. It had the look of a lawn furniture store from the outside, an unlovely affair with walls splashed with white paint, wedged between Pancho's Villa Mexican restaurant and a small parking lot. A short, stocky man with a goatee was sitting outside. The morning sun peeked over the far hills. Some hippie types in loose-fitting shirts and burdened with backpacks sashayed down the sidewalk. A distant train whistle blew mournfully.

I walked inside. There was an imploded look to the place. Some individuals in wheelchairs jostled along the hallways. Several people at the reception desk were hugging phones and talking animatedly. The white hallway walls were scuffed from wheelchairs whacking against them. They resembled retaining walls at auto racetracks, dirtied from cars slewing out of control. From an open office I heard a young woman, progressively going blind, tearfully unloading her problems to a counselor. I checked out some of the many notes thumbtacked to cork bulletin boards in the corridor. One read: "Disabled man seeks companion for headtripping, studying together, Scrabble, etc. Ray." Another: "For sale, one chrome wheelchair. Used for three months. $100. Call Peter." Another: "For sale. 1977 Dodge van. Built to drive from a wheelchair. Low mileage. Like new. Price: $10,000. Call Mike." Another: "Self-defense course. Become familiar with your own areas of strengths and weakness and how to apply these to self-defense techniques. The course will concentrate on using canes, crutches, and wheelchairs as tools in self-protection. Starting March 6." If you were disabled and needed help, this seemed the place to come.

The mover and shaker behind the center was an outspoken and vigilant man named Ed Roberts. In 1962, Roberts, a postpolio quadriplegic, became one of the first severely disabled students to attend the University of California at Berkeley. Not only was Roberts confined to a wheelchair, but he needed to spend most of his time inside an iron lung. He was put up at the Cowell Hospital on campus. Within a couple of years, Cowell became a haven for a dozen seriously disabled students in what had turned into a formal program, the Cowell Residence Program. The patients, however, found the hospital custodial in nature. They rarely ventured off campus into the community, the main reason being that the community was architecturally inaccessible to them. A unity developed, with a dim sense of purpose. They began to entertain the selfish, ambitious hope that they could get out of the hospital and live like the able-bodied.

They decided to whip up some alternative to the Cowell arrangement. With funds from the federal Office of Education, they created a Physically Disabled Students' Program in 1970. It was a sharp departure from past practice in medical and rehabilitation fields. The notion was to assume a hostile approach to society's limitations and to set up services directed at getting disabled people to live independent lives. The philosophy of the nine founding members was: Those who best know the needs of the disabled are the disabled themselves; comprehensive programs are urgently needed to meet those needs; disabled people must get out into the community. As the founders began to sculpt and implement programs, they found the disabled student population steadily swelling at Berkeley; more and more of these students began to move from Cowell into the community. Requests for help rose at an astonishing clip. Rarely were pleas turned away, even when they came from nonstudents. By the spring of 1971, the amount of time devoted to community people began to impinge seriously on the program's ability to meet the needs of students. Thus was hatched the idea of a separate Center for Independent Living to serve everybody. The particulars were hammered out for more than a year. The group was formally formed in April 1972. A roach-infested two-bedroom apartment was found with haste on, appropriately enough, Haste Street. The organization had one nagging problem: it had no money. Dollars were dug out of personal pockets, some benefit poker games were arranged, but not until July 1972 was the financial squeeze settled. The Rehabilitation Services Administration produced a grant for $50,000, enough to tide the center over while funds were secured from other sources. With a staff of a hundred and twenty people, half of them disabled, the center now serves about five thousand clients on an irregular basis.

My first stop was with the director of the blind services program. His name was Jon Sapunar, and I found him in a semilighted upstairs loft, the only area in the center not accessible to wheelchairs. He smiled in a placatory and friendly way. In his early thirties, he wore his hair at shoulder length and had on jeans and a work shirt, the center's operational garb. For the most part, the place is staffed by people in their twenties and thirties. Long hair and beards are predominant. Words like "dig," "cat," and "cool" are apparently part of everyone's vocabulary. Nonetheless, one member of the staff is an eighty-year-old man, a retired lawyer who once worked with Clarence Darrow, and who is stationed in the intake department fielding calls from first-time callers and explaining the center. But everyone had similar visions of how the world ought to be. Earnestness, sincerity, seems the order of the place.

"What most people think of as the blind are people who are totally blind," Sapunar told me. "Lots of people, more than you can shake a stick at, are partially blind. They have big problems, too, and we're interested in serving them."

Sapunar's eyes are set deep in their sockets, and I felt something peculiar about the way he stared at me, as if he weren't really looking at me but at something in the distance. I asked him about his own eyesight.

"Well, I'm legally blind," he said. "My vision is something like twenty–two hundred. To read, I use high-powered magnifying glasses, and to see traffic lights and all, I use this." He fished a small black eight-power monocular out of his pocket and held it up.

"I don't really know how to recognize faces," he said. "I can't distinguish your face. I see a dark object with two holes for eyes. Otherwise you're blurry. I can't see your mouth, but I know where it's at. If you were around a lot I'd recognize you by the smell of your jacket. It's a very strong smell. Or by your hairstyle. Not by your face. People walk around here, and those with vision like mine don't recognize them and they think we're stuck up or don't like them. So they get mad at us. The truth is that we just can't see them."

He continued, "When people come in here, I try to work at a functional definition of blindness. I ask people if they can see anything. Some people can only see light inside their head. That's a total. Others can tell day from night. But that's not very useful. Others have directionability. They can see a light and it tells them in what direction to go. That's the first level of usefulness. Then some people can see blurred objects and people. They can see a hand a few feet away. They can see light across the street. Recognize faces. That's getting into real usefulness."

I asked him what sort of people came for help.

Sapunar said that about a hundred people a month sought aid from the department, sometimes the same person returning a second or third time. "The leading cause of blindness today is diabetes," he said. "And the greatest part of the blind population is elderly, sixty-five or over. The people who come here reflect that."

One of the popular services Sapunar and his six assistants furnished was cane instruction. "Some people pick it up in an hour, some take weeks. We also try to teach people how to develop other senses. You can hear when traffic is coming. You can also feel in your body when you get near an object. Some totally blind people come in here and I don't even know they're blind because they use their other senses so well."

The department also acts as an advocate to push for changes in the community to help the blind. Most signs are too small for visually handicapped people to read. "We need large-print signs," Sapunar said. "Not big. Really big. Jumbo size. One of my problems is finding a bathroom. I can't distinguish between 'Men' and 'Women.' It's terribly embarrassing."

Jerry Wolf, who uses a walker to hobble about because of the crippling effects of multiple sclerosis, coordinates the housing department. A short, moon-faced man with glasses and a neat mustache, he was at a desk around the corner from the reception area, wrapping up a phone conversation with a client. "Yes, yes, we will do what we can. We are not God. Try to remember that."

The purpose of the department is to act as a listing agency of accessible housing for the disabled and as an advocacy group to prod landlords into making their housing accessible. The formidable hurdles it faces were expressed in black and white on a tattered map of Berkeley, tacked to the wall behind Wolf's desk. Shaded-in portions represented accessible housing. That meant six or less steps to get in. Most of the town, perhaps ninety percent, was unshaded. One reason was that a ramp to surmount just six steps could cost as much as a thousand dollars.

"The general vacancy rate in Berkeley is just one percent," Wolf said to me. "Finding wheelchair-accessible places cuts the supply down quite a lot. Anyway, rents are usually too high. They've gone up a good deal lately, so that a two-bedroom is two hundred dollars on up. Finding a studio under a hundred and fifty bucks is a feat of magic. We keep lists of people looking and try to arrange roommates. That's the only way some of these people can afford to put a roof over their heads." Wolf pointed out that although the dis-

abled can apply for housing subsidies, they're tough to get
and insufficient as yet to keep pace with demand.

Around a hundred requests a month were streaming into
the department, far too many to fill. "One of the problems we
have is that Berkeley is being advertised as a Utopia for the
disabled," Wolf said. "But not enough housing is available.
People are literally flocking here from all over the country.
They are landing at the airport and calling us up. About once
a month someone pulls up outside in a taxi with all his be-
longings and says, 'Here I am.' One person showed up with
an attendant and we had to put him in a hotel. His attendant
left and he started asking bellhops to empty his leg bag. The
hotel kicked him out. We finally found him a place with
another attendant. People commonly show up with no money.
One guy hitchiked here with his wheelchair. The rule is to
be totally unprepared."

Wolf shook his head. "The truth is, we're placing about
eight to ten people a month, though sometimes I'm surprised
that we place anyone at all."

I wondered how successful Wolf had been in convincing
landlords to make the modifications that would render
dwellings accessible to the disabled.

"Mixed success," he said. "A lot of landlords are reluctant
to do anything because they think ramps look ugly. Then
again, every so often we get a call from a landlord who wants
to rent to the handicapped. He likes them because the turnover tends to be low. One of the big problems is that no one
provides money for modifications. We try charitable organizations and private benefactors. We do get money sometimes, but not much. It's a case of twisting arms."

New housing, under law, is required to set aside a certain
number of apartments accessible to the handicapped. However, the law is useless if no housing is going up. Berkeley

hasn't seen any since 1973. Land is expensive; nobody is buying.

I walked outside and meandered through the parking lot to a cluster of garages. This was where the van-modification and wheelchair-repair departments were housed. Five gaily colored vans in need of repair were parked at the garage. Since the mid-1970s, more and more of the handicapped have purchased vans and modified them with lifts and hand controls so they could storm out onto the roads. One of the more popular programs at the center was the van-modification operation.

I threaded my way past the vehicles, my ears ringing from the sizzle of a welding torch that was sending out sparks. A man wearing a ski cap was poking underneath a gray van. He pounded its exhaust pipe with a rubber hammer. A shower of crud fell down on his head and down the neck of his striped coveralls. He stopped what he was doing and explained that about fifteen vans were being handled a month. Hand controls. Lifts. Special gates. Sliding seats. Power windows. A full conversion, he said, would take eight weeks and cost something like eight thousand dollars, less than most commercial places would charge.

The shop also superintends the center's own fleet of five vans, used to transport disabled and elderly people free of charge to wherever they care to go in the Berkeley area. As it happens, it's the center's most desired service, furnishing eighteen hundred rides a week. So great is demand that rides have to be reserved a week in advance.

At the far end of the garages was a shop where wheelchairs were fixed. Chairs were stacked all over. Manual chairs. Motorized chairs. A golf cart. The golf cart belonged to a young woman who can walk with canes and who breezes around town in the vehicle, carrying the canes in the back like golf clubs. Unfortunately, she got overzealous and crumpled the front end one day.

"We can fix most anything the same day," one of the men in the shop said. "You go to many places and they'll take weeks. Here, if we take any length of time, we have chairs to loan out so these people don't lose their mobility."

The shop performs emergency road service, something like an AAA of wheelchairs. The men can fix a flat in fifteen minutes. "The guys here are really reliable," the man said. "They may be at home on a weekend, bombed out of their minds, but when a call comes in they shoot right out there and fix it. Believe me, we get calls at all hours."

Eight repairmen work in the shop, three of whom sit in chairs themselves. The shop does about ten thousand dollars' worth of repair work a month. Wheelchair frames break constantly. "We do a whole lot of welding work," one of the men said. "A regular user may be in almost every week for repairs. These chairs are made terribly."

The durability of wheelchairs has long been a bone of contention among the handicapped. An estimated half-million disabled individuals rely on wheelchairs as their only means of locomotion, and their number is growing fast, yet a hill of complaints has arisen about the ruggedness of chair design. People have been hurled out of wheelchairs when wheels fell off. Chair motors and frames constantly break. Some have caught fire. And they are not cheap. Manual chairs generally sell for between three hundred and seven hundred dollars, and the increasingly popular battery-powered models fetch from a thousand to thirty-five hundred dollars. Disabled people I spoke with said that they often spend close to a thousand dollars a year to repair a motorized chair, and many of them find it necessary to keep a back-up chair so they don't sacrifice their mobility when one chair conks out.

For many years, the wheelchair market has been dominated by Everest and Jennings, a Los Angeles manufacturer that churns out some eighteen thousand wheelchairs a month. Some industry watchers figure that the company has captured a full two-thirds of the overall wheelchair market. Yet the E & J chair appears to have undergone relatively little modification since the basic design was conceived in 1913 by Harry Jennings, Sr., a mechanical engineer who fashioned the chair for his friend Herbert Everest, a mining engineer who lost his legs in a mine cave-in. The company didn't seem to alter the design very much when it added a heavy battery and a motor-controlling mechanism to produce a power chair in the mid-1950s.

Many complaints have been leveled against E & J. Its officials, for their part, bridle at any denunciation of their product. When I spoke to an executive there, he retorted that most of the problems with wheelchairs can be laid to one thing: maintenance. "People don't bother to maintain them properly, so they break down," he said. What's more, he said, wheelchairs are being used in ways they weren't used before, and it takes time to improve their durability. When I asked him about complaints over exorbitant costs, he replied that the industry wasn't unduly profitable, though he wouldn't divulge what the profit margin was on a chair (others have pegged it at fifty percent). Then he offered this curious analogy: "If you smoke, a pack of smokes is fifty cents. If you smoke two packs a day, that's a buck a day. If you have a manual chair and that chair lasts you five years, that's a quarter a day. That's pretty cheap."

In a small room off the center's chair shop toiled Vince Grippi, design engineer. Since late in 1975, he has been working to build the perfect wheelchair, a superchair. If he has his way, extant wheelchair manufacturers can go into the lawnmower business. His chair will be the best. Taped on the wall was a gigantic artist's rendition of the creation.

"You know, nobody has given a thought to the mobility of the handicapped," Grippi said, playing with a pencil. "Nobody cares about building a better chair. Well, I care. We talked to a lot of disabled people and most of them were unhappy with what they were sitting in. The speed, the range, the reliability, the flexibility. They really had no voice in what they needed. 'Here's a wheelchair,' they were told, 'take it or leave it.' Wheelchairs, you understand, are their legs. We started with a clean sheet of paper."

He pointed out some of the features of the superchair. It will have a cast frame that will be much sturdier. State-of-the-art technology will be incorporated. Grippi has designed an electric system that he claims will be much more reliable than conventional systems. "Most chairs will go four or five miles an hour and ten or twelve miles before the battery needs charging," he said. "Ours will go six miles an hour and thirty miles without charging. We've got a totally solid-state system, rather than a relay system."

The chair will be adjustable to handle any size person. With a traditional chair, you have to pull the arm rests out of the sockets and toss them on the floor to transfer out of the seat. In Grippi's chair, the rests will pivot downward electronically. The wheels are sturdier. And the chair is being constructed out of standard equipment that you can get anywhere. For instance, it uses Schwinn bicycle tires and an ordinary automobile battery. Everest and Jennings has its own tires and batteries. The chair is expected to be out sometime in 1980, at a cost of around $2,500. A comparable Everest and Jennings model, Grippi said, would cost $3,300.

❁   ❁   ❁

I ate dinner with Phil Draper and Judy Heumann — executive director and associate director, respectively, of the center. Both are quadriplegics. The typical discussion of where to go ensued. Everyone had his own favorite. A Chinese restaurant, Tung Yuen, was mentioned. Draper shrugged noncommittally. He said that would be okay, except he could fit under only one table there. Draper is tall. "Let's just hope we get it," he said. We were in luck. The table was vacant.

Heumann came down with polio when she was eighteen months old; she has been paralyzed from the shoulders down ever since. Draper has lived with other demons.

In 1961, Phil Draper was a fun-loving, carefree nineteen-year-old, interested in the same things most young men that age are interested in: girls, cars, booze. So it was not surprising that he and two friends set out in Draper's car on a weekend jaunt to Fairfield, California, near where he lived, to see what was happening there. Nothing was, as it turned out, so the trio turned around and headed home. There was beer in the car. Draper had two cans. He says he wasn't drunk; he could hold a lot more than that.

His memory stops three miles before the collision. For whatever reason, his mind has sealed away the secret, maybe because it is too ugly to recall. He was later told that it had been raining that night, but he remembers no rain. He was doing fifty-five when he jerked giddily to the right, crossed the divider, and slammed head-on into the onrushing car. The sound of the impact was like a bomb exploding. The engine from Draper's car was flung a hundred and fifty feet. One friend sailed out the rear window and miraculously escaped with minor injuries. The other friend was killed. A baby in the other car also died. Draper's neck was broken. He was left a quadriplegic. Investigators had little to work with. The car was a disfigured mound of metal. There was some indication that a tire might have blown out; or Draper just might have been reckless. No one is sure.

Draper spent most of three years in hospitals. Having been a bullheaded individual, he reacted to his disability with a combination of bitterness, depression, and resentment. Once he was released from the hospitals, he didn't get on with his parents, so he lived on his own with full-time attendant care. "This was back in the 1960s. It had never been heard of. It was a new experience. A vegetable living by himself." It wasn't much of a life, though. "I was far from active. I was thrust back into society as a freak. I lived an active life of doing nothing." For the most part, Draper drank. Beer. Wine. Hard stuff. Whatever he could get his hands on. He was drunk most of the time. The moments he wasn't, he mostly spent reading. He remembers one day reading every single word in the morning newspaper, including every word of advertising copy. "It was possibly the most boring experience in my entire life." He came to Berkeley in 1970 for no particular reason, learned about plans for an independent living center, got involved, and abandoned drinking. The center infected Draper with a rhythm for his life. He is thirty-eight now.

The Chinese restaurant was a tiny, dimly lit place. A half-dozen young people were crammed into the small room, their leathery faces and rumpled clothes blending with the dun-colored walls. Because of its proximity to the center, the restaurant often was patronized by the handicapped, and so fellow diners paid us no particular mind. Draper used a fork that was strapped to his wrist with an Ace bandage. But he could shovel food down pretty fast. The wheelchair doesn't disguise Draper's owlish, rabbinical bent. He speaks not with soapbox intensity, but softly, with an almost mournful tone.

I asked Draper and Heumann how they spent their time.

"The administration of CIL devotes most of its time to looking for money," Draper said unhappily. "It's a hard sell. It shouldn't have to be that way. We're not eating the money. This is a damned good cause. You find me a better one." The center was operating on a yearly budget of approximately $1.2 million, money extracted from about twenty-five different sources. "We have tapped every conceivable source," Draper said. "One of the biggest problems is that we have no permanent source for funding. So it's soft money. Most places fund for a year and that's it. Social service programs, as you might imagine, have a high mortality rate."

The bulk of the center's dollars have arrived in the form of grants from recognized government programs. It has also banged on the doors of just about every foundation in the Northern California area, with mixed results. Public service announcements are made on radio and TV. The quest has recently been expanded to the corporate world, and money has filtered in from Bank of America, IBM, Clorox, United Airlines, Kaiser Aluminum, and the like. "This is not yet a cause that has roused many people to open their wallets," Draper said. "You use every method by hook or crook to get the money. It's a constant hustle."

Staff salaries are kept to bare minimums. Counselors get about twelve thousand dollars. A coordinator of a program receives around fifteen thousand. Heumann gets a mere two hundred and fifty dollars a month, and Draper is paid three hundred and fifty. "So we can't very well be accused of lining our pockets," Draper said. "We would need about two hundred thousand dollars more to really pay our people what they could get in the marketplace." The average stay of a center staffer is three years. Some leave for money, but a good many leave to set up similar programs elsewhere, a move that the center encourages. A dozen or so centers have sprung up in other states, and the hope is that eventually they will blossom like mushrooms until there will be one in every metropolitan area.

I asked Draper and Heumann how they felt the movement was going.

"One thing that's very important," Draper said, "is the collectiveness, people working together. That's how they got their strength. Activism is found in only a few places in this country. We need more involvement. Too many disabled people are still sitting in their attics and reading old comic books. They've got to start shouting."

Heumann is a petite woman with a positive, earnest manner. She is thirty. She was once arrested on an airplane for refusing to get off after she and her wheelchair had been cleared to fly. She went to court and won.

"I think the movement lies in the hands of disabled individuals," she said. "I am concerned that not enough people understand the independent living programs. One of the reasons I think CIL is so successful is because it's run by disabled people. Our clients have hope when they see other disabled people managing their own lives. I don't know that the government is pleased that the disabled run these programs. Disabled people need to be much more militant about this. I think the next few years are going to be critical in the development of the movement. In a sense, the movement is just beginning."

I asked, are more demonstrations needed?

"More involvement," Draper said. "Just more involvement."

Heumann was crisp and downright. "We need more demonstrations. We still have many scores to settle."

Rain came and went the next morning. Somebody went putt-putting by on a motor scooter. The center's Law Resource Center is housed in a shopworn building across the street from the main building. I went there to talk to the program's director. Mismatched desks and chairs and bookshelves were spaced around the room. The floor was much scuffed up; track marks from wheelchairs were plainly visible. Old Congressional Records and Federal Registers were piled high on the floor. Coffee was percolating in a percolator. A spider plant was hanging in the window.

The director of the law center, Bob Funk, is a chunky, round-faced individual in his mid-thirties. He is a lawyer, one of two in the department. He walks with a pronounced limp. His left leg is not his. Funk was a Peace Corps volunteer when he got out of high school. He was shipped to Nigeria, where, in 1966, his skin inexplicably began to blister badly, and so he was flown to a hospital in Michigan. The disease, whatever it was, got progressively worse. His left leg was particularly bad. Doctors took it off. Tests came up with nothing that suggested what the problem might be. Funk grew sicker by the day. One afternoon, a pathologist assigned to his case was flipping through a medical journal. He came on an article about a rare disease that Africans were getting and dying from. It was called Mycobacterium Ulcerans, and it was related to tuberculosis and leprosy. Mmn, the pathologist wondered, could this be what Funk had? Tests were made. It was. "Had it not been for that article and for the fact that my doctor saw it when he did, I would have died," Funk said. He was the first Caucasian in the United States to contract it. As it was, no one knew of a medication to treat the disease. Operations were the only available source of relief, and Funk had thirty of them over a two-year period before he was finally cured. "After I got out, I was always denying my disability. I didn't like it. It was very depressing, very tearing, to go out in public and be stared at and pointed at." Yet he got through law school, heard the center needed a lawyer, and took the job.

We sat and talked in a small airless room.

"Our goal here is to be a backup to a lot of community groups," Funk said. "We're agitating to get the disabled to be more assertive. To have them know they can go out and raise hell."

A good deal of what the office does is explain the laws and rights of disabled people. It will also file suits and negotiate settlements. Funk said three suits were in court at the moment, and six were about to be filed. Three previous suits had already run their course, all successful for the center. Funk rattled off some recent cases. Three local restaurants wouldn't serve customers in wheelchairs. A waiter at one of them flatly said, "We don't serve wheelchairs." The second restaurant said it would serve the person if he sat in an isolated walkway that joined the place to a coffee shop. The third place refused service because it said the person was too disturbing a presence. He was in a wheelchair folded out like a bed. "Well, he would be disturbing," Funk said. "But that's tough. That's the law."

Complaints were reaching the center about auto insurance firms charging the handicapped thirty percent to fifty percent higher rates than the able-bodied, even though documentation makes clear they aren't greater risks. Funk said a class-action suit was being readied against one immense insurance firm.

"We are clearly in the right in almost every case we get," Funk said. "They're blatant cases of discrimination. Not even subtle discrimination. They haven't a chance in court. Discrimination is such a traditional thing in this country that these people don't even realize they're discriminating. We can't possibly lose most of these cases. In fact, we're forced into court a lot more often than we should be."

Funk laughed at the thought of how ridiculously simple most of the cases were. "What's likely to happen is that at first all of the cases will be blatant. Then they'll get subtler and subtler. People will get more sophisticated in their discrimination. Restaurants will refuse to serve a handicapped person but say the reason is that he's rowdy or doesn't have a tie on. The disability won't even be mentioned. This happened with the civil rights movement, and it took ten to twenty years to run its course. The same thing will happen with the handicapped."

Funk straightened up some papers on his desk, shifted in his seat. He said, "What we need is more action, more attorneys to bring suits and more disabled people to go out and be aggressive. Lots of disabled people are being discriminated against and are just accepting it and not telling anybody about it. If all this discrimination is taking place in Berkeley, the supposed liberal bastion, then it surely is happening all over the country."

Anne Steiner is a beautiful girl with raised eyebrows and poignant circles of pure white skin around her eyes. Her only disability is a bad case of arthritis. She's in her thirties and has an infirmity most people don't get until their sixties. She heads the center's job development program, which faces the awesome task of trying to get jobs for the disabled.

When I found Steiner in her cluttered office, she was finishing up with some visitors from the Japanese embassy. They were checking out the center with a mind toward starting one in Japan. They were scurrying around in their blue sports jackets and dark ties, cameras slung around their necks. One of them was asking a man suffering from muscular dystrophy if he could please pose using a gooseneck phone. "This will be a wonderful picture," the Japanese man said. "Okay," the muscular dystrophy man said. "But I haven't shaved."

"Basically we're a placement service," Steiner said to me.

"Somebody has to come in here with some education, skills, abilities that could be translated into jobs. We've had lawyers. We've had a person who was a missionary. We've had a talented artist. We're mostly working with the physically handicapped, but we're expanding into the mentally handicapped."

The program has a caseload of a hundred and twenty-five clients, Steiner said. Since the program began in the fall of 1975, the placement rate has hovered around forty percent, she said, though it had of late nudged up to sixty percent.

She spoke of some unusual cases. A blind janitor had been placed in a nearby town. "This was one of the cases where I said, no way, there's just no way for this one." The man told Steiner that he had experience scrubbing his father's laundromat. He was totally blind in one eye and legally blind in the other. How would he clean a room? He said he would scout out the premises in advance until he knew the area by memory. How would he tell what was dirty and what was clean? He said he would assume everything was dirty and clean it all. Steiner said that a man with muscular dystrophy got a job doing drafting for the Navy. The only necessary concession was a lower drafting table.

"We work a lot with employers, too," Steiner said. "Basically, we try to advocate for the disabled in general. We don't go in and say, 'Hey, you're really stupid the kind of attitude you have.' We're subtler than that. We generally work with personnel people who are sympathetic because they don't have to work with the handicapped people. We'll do whatever is needed to help the employers. We'll check out the work environment to see what modifications are necessary. We'll help draft affirmative action plans. We're getting a lot more interest from employers worried about the law."

❄ ❄ ❄

I strode through the hallways of the center for a while. The place still mumbled with wheelchairs. I moved against the wall to let a particularly chunky man in an oversized wheelchair slip past. I nodded and said, "How are you?" "Couldn't be better," the man boomed. "It's a great day to be alive." After you've been there for some time, the center begins to have a curious effect on you. Seeing nothing but disability, of every sort imaginable, hearing how one can be stricken under the most innocent of circumstances, I began to wonder how it was that anyone was able-bodied. Of course, the handicapped have the exact opposite feeling when they are out and about in society. They are often the only disabled people in sight, and they wonder how it is that anyone could be handicapped.

Tanya Temporal, a counselor in the research and demonstration project, sat on top of a desk on the first floor, beneath the blind services department. She was finishing a staff meeting. Temporal counsels severely disabled people. The project she is a part of hopes to prove that peer counseling of the handicapped works better than any other kind. Her short frame and lean, cheerful face belonged in California, I thought. Her hair, wild and electric, looked fine in Berkeley. She was in her early twenties, and was prematurely gray. Her conversation is a stream of information, a Niagara of words, that, even so, somehow seems laconic. She smiles quickly and steadily.

"One of the main things we do is emotional counseling," she told me. "Getting people to deal with their disability and to accept it. We have five part-time counselors, and each one handles about ten clients. We have a caseload all together of about eighty clients."

She talked about her most difficult case at the moment: A twenty-three-year-old girl afflicted with severe cerebral palsy who lived in an institution. Her speech is extremely difficult to understand. Tanya worked with her for two months before beginning to comprehend. Tanya's charge is apprehensive about moving out of the institution, not being sure she has the skills to venture into the world.

"I'm dealing with her on an emotional level," Tanya said. "I'm not really telling her. I'm allowing her to discover. A lot of time we role-play. 'Okay, here we are in your apartment. I know you like to bowl. Let's go over how you'll set up a bowling appointment. Who are you going to call?' I've got to get her to demand to go out and do things, not wait around for others to ask. She hasn't really accepted her disability. She views it as a burden that God has placed on her. She believes that by God's magic power she'll recover some day. She's very religious. I try not to discourage that belief altogether. I try to tell her, okay, for today you're not going to get better. What can we do today?"

Tanya gave out one of her affectionate smiles. "I'm also doing some sexuality counseling with her. She really wants to be with a mate. She's deformed. Her body is small and her legs are twisted. I'm having her do body appreciation. I make her say, 'This is my leg. I love my leg.' When she can love her body, then someone else can love her and appreciate her, not before. I've been counseling her for six months, and she's still depressed a lot. She whines and cries. She's threatened suicide a couple of times. She's slowly getting better, but I don't think she can get into an independent living situation until she gets herself together. It's hard to say how far away from that she is."

Tanya studied human development in college. For thirteen years, she has suffered rheumatoid arthritis. She has no idea why she got it. She has no pain, but has trouble walking and holding things. She occasionally resorts to a wheelchair. "I have accepted my disability," she said. "I can't say I don't get angry when I drop something on the floor and can't pick it up. But I don't let anger overtake me. I'm not going to paint the picture of the super crip. Some people make it out that they're the super crip and it's wonderful to be disabled. Well, that's going overboard the other way. It's never wonderful to be disabled. But you can still be a whole person. You can still be a happy person."

I went next to another hive to chat with Lon Kuntze. He, too, was in his early twenties, a big broad-shouldered man with frizzy hair and a beard. Deaf since birth, he runs the deaf services program. He nodded hello when I came by. Lynette Taylor, the center's staff interpreter, was to assist in our interview, though she was preoccupied with some phone calls. Kuntze suggested we begin by writing questions and answers on a legal pad.

"The biggest problem for deaf people," he wrote, "is of course communications. The deaf are the only disabled group that can't regularly use the phone."

The only way the deaf can talk, Kuntze explained, is by use of what are known as TTYs. Basically old teletypewriters that, by use of a jack, can be hooked to a phone line, they clack out in written form what conversation is to be exchanged. They aren't cheap and they aren't readily available, so even if a deaf person could get hold of one, he couldn't call very many people. Some federal offices have installed them, as has the phone company at a few of its service centers. One of the troubles is that it's an agonizingly slow way to talk, yet anyone talking over a TTY pays standard phone rates. A popular deaf person can run up some gigantic bills.

Lynette finished with her calls, and came over to interpret.

Her mother was deaf, so she picked up sign language early on. Kuntze said he was relieved; he was getting a writing cramp.

"Deafness is totally a disability on the communications level, whereas other disabilities are on a physical level," Kuntze said. "The deaf can't deal with people who don't know sign language. The best remedy for the communications problem is interpreters. The biggest trouble is there aren't enough interpreters, and there's no money for interpreters. Interpreters. Interpreters. Interpreters. Interpreters cost up to ten dollars an hour. Most of them get seven-fifty. Court work gets them fifteen dollars. The money, from their standpoint, is terribly low. It should be equal to foreign language interpreters, who get fifteen to thirty-five dollars an hour. That's why more interpreters haven't been attracted to the field. Deaf interpreters simply don't get a decent wage."

My last visit was with the community affairs department. Its aim is to address community issues and to inspire demonstrations when it senses the need. I spoke with Kitty Cone, who has muscular dystrophy, and with Hale Zukas. Zukas's cerebral palsy is so severe that he has but limited use of his hands and can barely utter intelligible speech. A slender man with a wild bush of red hair that tumbled down to his shoulders, Zukas is in his mid-thirties. Because he can't use his hands to steer his wheelchair, he wears a heavy headband with an attached pointer. This, touched to a contact on the arm of the chair, plus a flipper his one good foot can maneuver, can control his course. The pointer is also his second voice. Even associates have trouble understanding him, and those first meeting him find his slow, broken utterances impossible to decipher. So Zukas devised a conversation board — a chart of letters and figures and frequently

used words (he, she, they, were, over, should, move, there).
When he gets bogged down, he spells out his thoughts with
a brisk tapping of the pointer. The back of his wheelchair
sports a button reading: "ACCESS AMERICA."

Of late, the department had been working at mobility and
architectural issues. Thumbtacked on the wall were two
immense maps, one of Berkeley and one of Oakland. Black
dots were inked in where ramps or curb cuts had been
made. Berkeley looked pretty good, but Oakland had a long
way to go before it could be called an accessible city.

"We are working quite a bit on transportation issues,"
Kitty said.

Hale began to struggle, wanting to say something. I
couldn't understand his grunting. Saliva drooled down his
beard and onto his clothes. Kitty had to interpret. "Hale
says, 'Boy do we work on transportation. We're suing everybody in the world.'"

Paramount to all severely disabled people is the issue of
getting around. For long distances, matters have improved
since the Federal Aviation Administration ruled in May
1977 that airlines can't deny seats to handicapped individuals.
It had been common practice for the airlines to boot disabled people off planes, contending that they might hamper
evacuation procedures should there be an emergency. Now
all airline personnel are required to be properly schooled
in ways of handling the disabled. Several cruise ships have
started to take wheelchair travelers. The first ocean liner so
designed, the *Queen Elizabeth II*, boasts nine staterooms
that were made for the disabled, with twelve more that are
accessible to them. Thirteen elevators are on the ship. Some
of Amtrak's trains can accommodate wheelchairs in certain
bedrooms and these trains offer accessible bathrooms. Stations are being built barrier-free. Hertz and Avis have hand

control cars at some of their locations, and the newer highway rest areas accommodate the handicapped. For lodging, Holiday Inn is making one in every hundred rooms accessible to the disabled population.

Local travel, though, is something else again. Wheelchair users can't very well hop into taxis. Subways, with the exception of the San Francisco, Washington and Atlanta lines, aren't available to the severely disabled. And no realistic evidence suggests they ever will be. Elevators would be needed, and they cost a staggering amount. Public buses aren't much better, since their floors are around thirty-five inches above street level. A protracted battle, involving a spate of suits by handicapped groups, resulted in an order in May of 1977, from Transportation Secretary Brock Adams, requiring that buses with twenty-two-inch floors — called Transbuses — be produced by 1979. Twenty-two inches is about as low as buses can be made, without having them scrape the ground when climbing hills or going over bumps. The buses would also have to include ramps that would shoot out from underneath to allow wheelchairs and mobility-hampered individuals to come aboard. The handicapped, however, aren't ablaze with enthusiasm over Transbuses. For one thing, the low-floor buses won't start rolling down city streets until 1981 or 1982, and a complete transition will take a good deal longer. The old buses must first wear out. What's more, how are the handicapped people going to get from their homes and offices to the nearest bus stops?

The center was in the midst of a suit against AC Transit, the biggest bus line in the Berkeley area, for failing to order accessible buses, as required by a California law, as well as by the federal order. AC owns a fleet of about eight hundred buses. As I talked with Kitty and Hale, a big AC bus rumbled past outside.

"Let us ride your bus," Kitty shouted out the window.

Hale laughed loudly and nodded his head in agreement with the sentiment.

Another transportation issue had to do with BART. One of the three accessible subway systems in the country, BART was planning to automate a lot of its stations by withdrawing agents and monitoring stations through closed-circuit TV. The disabled were aghast at the prospect. They sometimes needed help to pay their fares, and if someone has an epileptic seizure or a blind person falls on the tracks, no agent would be available to assist. The main issue is safety, though, since the disabled fear that muggings and rapes would climb at an alarming rate. So Kitty and Hale were orchestrating protests to pressure BART into abandoning the idea. Pickets and rallies were being planned.

"We don't want to badmouth BART, because they are accessible to us," Kitty said. "But this just isn't going to happen. No automation. Automation is for the birds."

Kitty then related a horrifying story that illustrated the inequities in the benefits system for the handicapped. A twenty-seven-year-old woman named Lynn Tompson, afflicted by muscular dystrophy, lived with an attendant in Los Angeles. The pain from her disease was so bad that her legs had to be disconnected from her hips. Most of her medical expenses were being picked up by Supplemental Security Income payments. In general, Social Security laws define a disabled person as someone who can't engage in "substantial gainful activity." Such activity, according to these laws, is any enterprise generating an average income of two hundred dollars a month over a nine-month stretch. That means that someone who can't budge a muscle below his chin, but who holds a job paying a mere two hundred dollars a month, isn't disabled in the eyes of the law, and thus isn't eligible for the SSI program or for Medicaid and other benefits. It's a rotten system, the handicapped agree.

Without paying staggering premiums, severely disabled people can't get conventional medical coverage. The architects of the welfare laws plainly never imagined that severely handicapped people might earn a salary. Under current laws, they would have to either make a fairly scant income and get benefits to help out or else earn a hefty salary.

Lynn Tompson wasn't happy sitting in her apartment and rotting away. So she started working as a dispatcher. She enjoyed hearing other people's voices and felt good about accomplishing something. Eventually, she worked her way up to an income of five hundred dollars a month, hardly enough to meet all her bills by itself, but she was gaining some freedom. Social Security people stopped in one day to check up on her and discovered her extra income. She hadn't reported it to them. Her payments were immediately cut off. What's more, she was notified that she owed ten thousand dollars in back payments that had been made to her. The only way she could live would be to go to a nursing home. Instead, in February of 1977 she committed suicide. She left a note saying that her death could be blamed on Social Security.

One of the cruel ironies of the case was the fact that, unbeknownst to Lynn, California had recently passed a measure allowing handicapped people to draw medical coverage, as well as funds to pay for home nursing care, while they're working. The law established a graduated scale, so that beyond a certain income a person chips in part of his expenses and the state furnishes the rest. Handicapped groups are trying to persuade other states to follow the California precedent.

"The tragedy of this story," Kitty said, "is that Lynn Tompsons can be found all over the country. California has done something to rectify the benefits problem, but what are other states doing? The handicapped must scream at their legislators to start moving, because the laws are sending us to psychological deaths."

Early the next morning, I caught a plane out of San Francisco, leaving the center behind. Beyond doubt, I had returned to the "real" world. I checked carefully the passengers aboard my crowded United Airlines flight. Not one was disabled.

5

I FOUND Tommy Trussell at the Shell Station at 73rd and Indiana. He was making change for a big, puffy-faced man who was wearing a white cowboy hat. This was Lubbock, a flat, dusty spider of a town in West Texas. Tracts of little houses bunched close together. Mobile homes. They sell quarter horses here. It was getting on toward dusk and it was broiling hot.

Trussell slid the change across the counter and the man scooped it up in a meaty palm. "Thank you now," Trussell said. "You hurry right back and see us."

The man lumbered out the glass door and, gazing out reflectively from behind the elevated counter at the pumps outside, Trussell drummed his fingers against his chair and just smiled. "Hot," he said. "Oh golly, how it's hot. You just sort of wish you were water."

To anyone sailing in and out of the station, Tommy Trussell's limitations aren't very obvious. His speech is fluent enough, though it's liberally sprinkled with clichés and with expressions he uses in irritating repetition. While he's hunched behind the counter at the filling station, you don't see the immobile right arm and leg. You have to talk with him a bit before you begin to realize that something is wrong. Tommy Trussell's I.Q. is seventy-eight, low enough to qualify him as a borderline retardate.

Workers were flocking from their jobs into the heat, so cars started to pound into the Shell station one after the other. It's self-service. Once you pump in what you need, you go into a cramped, glass-sided office to pay Trussell. BankAmericard or Master Charge will do. Trussell has gotten good at tearing off credit card receipts with one hand.

"Lord, sometimes I barely have a moment to breathe during the busy hour," he said. "But I sure do like it. I like meeting the people. I sure do meet a lot of different people. Interesting people. I am just awfully glad to be out of that state school."

Trussell was born William Thomas Yates, the son of a seventeen-year-old runaway in a home for unwed mothers in Sauk Center, Minnesota, around ninety miles northeast of Minneapolis. That was in 1946. His mother was an alcoholic and didn't care to raise him. For a brief period, he lived with his maternal grandmother in a dilapidated section of Minneapolis. She didn't care much for him, either. In December 1951, she got mad at him — he can't remember why — and looped a nametag around his neck and shipped him off, at the age of four, on a thousand-mile train journey to Vernon, Texas, where his mother lived. His mother forced him to sleep on the floor. On Christmas Eve, just three weeks after his arrival, the night was so bitterly cold that he tried to crawl into bed with his mother to warm up. She exploded with rage. As punishment, she yanked him out of bed by his feet, bouncing his head on the floor. Then she made him get on the bed and pulled him off again. Next she hurled him against a chair and pounded him on the head with a big cooking fork until he was unconscious. The beating badly damaged his brain. It left his right arm and leg paralyzed.

He spent two years in hospitals recuperating, and underwent several brain operations. His mother was sent to prison.

The case attracted a wash of national publicity. Sacks of letters poured in to the judge who had taken custody of Trussell, hundreds of them from couples anxious to adopt him. Custody was awarded to Mr. and Mrs. J. H. Trussell, a middle-aged couple living in Hale Center, Texas, just north of Lubbock. Their young son had recently died of polio. The husband was then a section foreman on the Santa Fe Railroad. They adopted him in April 1953 and changed his name to Tommy Vernon Trussell. Six years went by with the Trussells trying hard to persuade themselves that nothing was wrong with Tommy other than a useless arm and leg. Yet by the time he turned twelve, the facts were undeniable. He was still stuck in the third grade and seemingly not trying very hard to get to the fourth. He became difficult to control. In school he was impossible. He would cruise around the classroom, chattering, clutching at the girls, calling the teacher "dreamboat" and "babe" and "honey." Trussell was given psychological tests and was found to possess an I.Q. of only fifty-one, meaning he was functioning at the level of an average six-year-old. He was classified as moderately retarded and committed to the state school at Abilene. Later, so that he could be closer to the Trussells, he was transferred to a new state school at Lubbock. Needless to say, sending him away broke the Trussells' hearts. They kept up hope, but they didn't expect to live to see the day when he got out of those schools.

Oddly enough, Trussell began to improve. School psychologists were completely baffled. They suspected that perhaps other parts of his brain were gradually taking over for the damaged areas. Steadily, his I.Q. crept higher, until it finally settled at seventy-eight. That left Trussell in a below-average range known as "borderline." For twenty years, his teachers patiently drilled him in tasks that a normal eighth-grader does routinely. Telling time. Making change. Fixing the bed. But with repetition, Trussell not only picked them up, but he got the hang of elementary reading, writing, and math. His emotional problems began to lessen. Stuck in institutions most of his life, Trussell had learned that the way to get what he wanted was to throw a temper tantrum. It took years to rid him of that attitude. When he would get mad, he would be ordered to mop the floor. Once he was locked up. "I was real mean back yonder. I began to see in time that if I did what they told me to, I'd make it on the outside. I learned that they were the boss and I'd better start minding them so I could get out." Instead of throwing fits, Trussell began to scribble letters to the school newspaper and stuff ideas into the campus suggestion box. The Lubbock school used to play music around the clock to soothe the babies there. "I couldn't sleep with any music. So I wrote letters saying to cut out that music. They did turn it down some. I told them that if they didn't I was going to go and sleep in the bathroom."

In 1971, Trussell was enrolled in a job-training program at the school. He was started on the road to independence. It was a painful four-year process. First he had to live in a special dorm on campus, which he shared with other retardates. Trussell talked all the time about getting out on his own. But he found that acquiring the ways of independent life was hard. He struggled to do tasks, to remember actions familiar to most people. He was tortured and teased about his inability to remember. Sometimes he got terribly depressed, wrapped up in his own misery. He went to special classes to acquire the everyday skills he would need to have outside the institution. How to balance a checkbook. How to cook and plan meals. How to deal with pushy salesmen ("They told me to just stand my ground or else I'd end up buying everything there was to buy"). How to find the rest-room in public buildings ("I was to just go and ask some-body").

In December of 1975, Trussell at long last settled down in an apartment which he shares with two roommates, both retarded, who still attend the state school. Shortly afterward, he was formally discharged from the school. "They can't ever take me back now. I'm permanently loose."

During all those years, Trussell was being taught voca-tional skills to support his independence. Much of the lessons had to do with so-called work tolerance training, jobs whose principal virtue was that they gave Trussell something he had to do regularly. He helped bathe, feed, and do laundry for the school's dozens of profoundly retarded residents, whose low intelligence barely enabled them to breathe, swallow, and defecate. Five cents an hour was his wage. The work so disgusted him that he quit six times. "I kept coming back, 'cause I knew that if I wanted to get out of that school I had better learn something. They weren't going to let me out to do nothing. That, I was pretty sure of."

In time, Trussell found jobs off campus. He tried his hand at selling lightbulbs by telephone at a business that em-ployed only handicapped workers. The bulbs were guaran-teed for five years, but customers were complaining that they were burning out inside of five months. The owner shut the business down. Trussell was hired to pack spices into cellophane bags. His pay was ten cents for a dozen bags. He was fired for being too slow. "It didn't seem fair. There were some old hags working there, and they were allowed to take their sweet old time putting the spices in. But I got hollered at." Next, he got a job at a gas station. It was managed by a man married to a helper at the state school. Both Trussell and the man loved wrestling and used to watch matches together. But what the couple really was after was Trussell's money. Friends and strangers who had heard about his case had contributed money to someday get him on his feet; a trust fund of about fifteen hundred dollars accumulated. That would be his as soon as he was discharged from the school. At the station, Trussell was forced to work fifteen hours a day, seven days a week. He was supposed to get fifty cents an hour, but he rarely pocketed more than thirty dollars a week. Some weeks he got nothing. What's more, every time he took a bad check or credit card, the owner would ask him to write out a check. Usually Trussell refused. Finally, one night the owner got roaring drunk and threatened to harm Trussell if he didn't write out a check for two hundred and fifty dollars. He did. Later that night, he called his mother. A social worker from the school arrived the next day, retrieved the check, and convinced Trussell he should quit. "I saw that the man was taking advantage of me. But I wanted out of the school, so I knew I had to hold a job of some kind."

He worked briefly at another filling station. When the station hired him, however, they didn't know about his physical limitations. They wanted someone who could change a tire, put in fresh oil, wash cars. So Trussell was dismissed after a few days. A couple of weeks later, he found the job at the Shell station. He works the night shift, two-thirty to ten, and gets the minimum wage. His boss likes him because he's highly reliable and honest. Although he occasionally makes mistakes, the boss tends to overlook them.

Not long after I visited Trussell, I sought out his adoptive mother, Lora, and talked to her about the life he has made for himself. She said, "We're just so happy about it, we don't hardly know what to do. When we adopted him, we didn't know whether he was ever going to walk or talk. He was in braces then and he could say just five words: 'mama,' 'dadda,' 'go,' 'home,' and 'bite.' 'Bite' tended to get the heaviest use. He always seemed to want a bite of something. He didn't make it at all in the public schools. It seemed that he felt the world was his and he could run it. He didn't believe he had to mind anybody but me and the husband. When he was committed to the state school, we figured that that was the only place he'd ever make it. The Lord has been sweet to us, though, and when our time is up, we know he can make his way in life. We have no fears about him. He does his own banking, grocery shopping, going to church, cab paying, what anybody else does. He's a regular citizen. He's got no serious gripes or bellyaches. He was home just the other weekend, and I was having so gosh much trouble opening this jar. I said to him, 'Could you hold this jar for me while I twist it?' No, he said, he'd do it himself. So he went and squatted down on the floor and clamped the jar between his knees and opened that lid with his good hand. No sir, we're not uneasy about him making his way."

A podgy man with a heavily wrinkled face came in, paid Trussell, and asked if there was a sink where he could wash his hands.

"Why, I believe there's one in the ladies' room," Trussell said, and he started to fish for the key.

"Ain't no way I'm going into any ladies' room," the man grumbled. He left.

Trussell had on a white short-sleeved shirt decorated with green palm trees, and brown plaid pants. He is a slight man, about five-foot-six and 130 pounds. He wears his hair combed in a way to hide the scars of his brain operations. He holds his right arm in a bent position across his waist. The fingers are wrapped together. He shakes hands with his left hand. He almost always wears a smile on his face. At the counter in front of him were a machine for imprinting credit cards on charge slips, a rickety adding machine, and a console with switches for controlling the six pumps. A Coke machine stood in the corner, some mops leaning against it, and a row of cardboard holders with maps stood on the window ledge.

The job is a simple one and hardly varies from one customer to the next. Trussell reads the amount of gasoline used on the console and collects the money for it. The hardest part of the day comes after the station shuts down, when Trussell has to read the pumps and compute the total amount of gas sold during his shift and the total price paid for it. Even with the adding machine, weeks of practicing were necessary before Trussell mastered bookkeeping. "Oh golly, I had to have the boss come down here three or four times a week at first to bail me out. It sure was hard. But I got it down. Sure did." He laughed. He has a splendid, shoulder-shaking laugh that is very infectious.

Trussell gets by. His work would bore most people. At best, they would see it as a temporary expedient. Trussell is loud in his praise for it. He seems to find a mesmerism in the selling, in the coins and the bills and the all-day touching of hands. "No sir," he told me. "I haven't any plans to leave the station. I like station work. When I got to wait a half hour or so between customers, I might get a little bored. But hardly ever. I believe I was made for station work."

Trussell gave the wrong change to a middle-aged woman in hiking shorts. She demanded her extra dollar. "You give me my dollar, mister."

"I'm sorry," Trussell said. "I forgot. Here is your dollar. Now, have a good day."

She didn't believe Trussell's mistake a mistake, and walked away in a huff. At the door, she turned and glowered. She moved on.

Trussell has a small Magnavox black-and-white TV that

is always kept on, perched on a shelf beside him. He rarely reads anything, though he's able to understand simple newspaper stories. For the most part, he's content to watch the tube. Trussell will watch anything, though he's especially partial to quiz shows and "shoot-'em-up movies." He likes to see good conquer evil.

An Ajax commercial blared out from the set, and Trussell looked up. I asked him about the pitfalls of living on his own. "I sure make lots of mistakes," he answered. "One time I remember I put the rubber doormat into the dryer and it came pretty close to burning up. My parents had come over that night and they smelled something and took it out before it caught fire. They said it would be better if I didn't put it in there anymore." Another time, he said, he threw a Shake 'n Bake package into the oven and waited around for a chicken to appear. All that appeared was a burnt Shake 'n Bake package. He's gotten better with time. Each morning, he's able to cook his own breakfast, choosing from french toast, pancakes, or a couple of eggs. He's adept at cracking an egg with one hand. After work, he usually pops a frozen dinner into the oven.

His atrophied right leg makes it hard for him to get around. He used to own a large tricycle, but was worried about driving it at night to work, so he sold it. The filling station is four miles from his apartment. No bus runs along the route, so he has to take a cab to and from work. The cab costs him roughly a hundred and twenty dollars a month, close to forty percent of his take-home pay. Most of the rest of his money goes to keep a roof over his head and food in the refrigerator. He goes to maybe one movie a year when he has the cab fare. Once a week or so he eats at a fast-food restaurant across the street. He has no interest in women. Every Sunday, he attends the Smithlawn Church of Christ, and once or twice a day he phones his parents, who live ten miles away in Slaton. And he does a lot of walking.

"People think that somebody like me can't make it out on his own," he said to me. "But, as you can see, I'm making it. It's not always easy, but I'm making it. People sometimes take advantage of me. Some of them tease me. They say, 'There goes crip. There goes that crip.' But I tell them I can probably do more with one hand than they can with two."

Trussell's memory is short. He forgets names. He had to think hard to remember the names of his roommates, and even though I had spoken with him several times before, he kept forgetting who I was and where I was from. In introductions to several people, I was variously from Fort Worth, Chicago, Los Angeles. Never New York.

I asked him about the state school.

"There were some good points and some bad points," he said. "The state school is not where I would really want to make my home. The Lubbock state school helped me in a lot of ways, but I sure wouldn't want it to be my home. Just the words 'state school' didn't sound right to me. They rubbed me the wrong way. Before I went to the school I had privileges. Once I went there I had those privileges taken away. That didn't seem the way things ought to be done."

He nodded. He nods a lot when he talks.

"I had my doubts whether I would ever get out, but I thought some day I might. I got depressed lots of times. When they began to put me in sheltered living and halfway houses I began to think there just might be a job out there for me and I just might get out on my own."

Does he resent his original mother? I asked.

"I sure do," he said immediately. "It wasn't right what she did. It wasn't right that she beat me. I only wanted to get warm." His mother has been released from prison, though

Trussell has not seen or talked to her since the night of the beating.

A young man came in and paid for three dollars and eighty-five cents' worth of gas all in change. Trussell needed a while to count the coins and to slip them into their appropriate slots in the money drawer.

Ten o'clock. Closing time. Trussell went out to read the pumps. He walks with a lopsided gait. He is a shuffler, lifting his left foot against the pressure of his right, sliding hesitantly forward in little whispering movements. The smell of spilled gas was pungent. The pumps showed that he had sold twelve hundred and twenty-five gallons of regular, eight hundred and ninety-two gallons of unleaded, and a hundred and ninety-six gallons of Super Shell. He jotted down the figures on a pad, then shuffled back inside and proceeded to do the books, toting things up on the Olivetti adding machine that hummed as it performed its calculations. His take for the day came to $1,271.12.

"That's a pretty darn good day," he said. "I have done better. One Friday here I sold five thousand gallons. Boy, that was something to see. But I got no complaints about today. Sure don't."

He swept together a stack of money, credit card slips, and his day's report and stuffed them into a gold pouch. He zipped the pouch shut with his teeth. Then he lumbered over to a safe in the floor near the door and stashed the pouch inside.

I drove Trussell the four miles to his apartment. Patches of streetlight dappled the road. We passed by a group of boys in their early teens playing baseball on a weed patch set among some warehouses. Sodden people with wine bottles in paper bags sat in big broken cars outside one of the warehouses. Stardust Apartments wasn't much. It was a two-level affair with flaking paint in places, weeds grown too tall. Trussell was on the second floor. Shoulders seesawing, he struggled up the steps. He was winded and wheezing by the time he got to the top. As he opened the door, one of his roommates, Jimmy, was sitting on a chair with a small light on, listening to a radio through an earplug. Lights are kept to a minimum to save on electricity. Jimmy nodded hello. He worked at a Big Texas Steak Ranch, scrubbing dishes. The third roommate, Danny, was asleep. He worked an early shift washing cars.

The living room was an unlovely mixture of mismatched furniture. On the inside of the door was a Dallas Cowboys cheerleader poster. Dirty laundry was stacked in a basket in the middle of the room, and nearby was Jimmy's bike. Trussell gave me a tour of his room, a tiny box with a single bed. Paper grocery bags covered the floor. Trussell liked to store things in bags rather than closets. "I don't know why. Just do."

A sign on his bedroom door read, "Don't sleep in my bed, and if you do make it up." I asked him about the sign and he winced like a man sucking an aching tooth. He explained that a person he had known from the state school used to come by and harass him and mess up his bed. "I don't let him in here anymore. We chase him away."

I asked Jimmy when he had begun work. He said, "November 15, 1974, at one o'clock."

Does he like it?

"I sure do. They're pretty happy with me. I work right hard."

I asked Trussell what he does after work. "Oh, me and Jimmy sit here and talk a bit," he said. "I tell Jimmy how many gallons of gas I sold today. He tells me how many dishes he washed. That may sound silly, but that's what we do. We watch a little TV and then go to bed."

We sat there for a spell, the room quiet, the light barely

enough for us to see each other. Jimmy was nervously puffing on a cigarette. Trussell was poking with a pen at the dining room table. Two eight-year-old minds in men's bodies. It was midnight, so I said I ought to be going. Jimmy nodded good-bye. Trussell stuck out his left hand.

He said, "Now, you ever get back this way, you drop in, you hear? I got an extra blanket and a pillow, so we can put you up good on the couch."

I told him I'd be sure to do that.

"It's nice here," Trussell said. "We sure are having a good time, aren't we, Jimmy?"

"Yeah, that sure is right," Jimmy said.

6

In Boston, I visited the William M. Trotter School, Barbara Jackson principal, 135 Humboldt Avenue, Roxbury. It was one of the first schools in the country to go about mainstreaming the handicapped in a major way. It's a lovely school. It's new, it's clean, it's well lit. Two stories of brick. Modernistic. Yellow school buses shuddered to a stop outside, and boisterous children jumped out and raced for the doors. The children seemed exuberantly at home. One child had to be pushed. He was in a wheelchair. Another small boy limped along on crutches. Grades kindergarten through fifth are taught here. An elevator inside takes disabled students to the second floor.

It was Friday afternoon, cloudy but warm, and after I looked in on a few classes for a while and talked with Jackson, I spent some time with Barbara Fagone, first- and second-grade teacher, pressing like any visitor for an understanding of how mainstreaming was going. She is a cheerful, conversational woman with short brown hair.

"These kids, for the most part, have never seen a handicapped child before," she said. "So naturally they at first react with a burst of curiosity. 'Why can't he walk? Why does he talk so funny? When's he going to hop out of that wheelchair? How's that chair work, anyway?' All that lasts about twenty minutes, till it's explained to them. I tell them that, just as they get sick sometimes with a cold, these children are sick in a different way. Some of them can't walk. Some have other problems with their bodies. But that doesn't mean you can't play with them. It doesn't mean they can't learn just like you. I try to press the idea that this isn't something uncommon. That when you go downtown shopping or out to eat, you're going to see people like this. It's part of life. No big deal. Kids this age are so flexible that they just nod and get on with their business."

Fagone has been teaching this kind of integrated class since 1974. That was the year when a bill to guarantee equal education for the handicapped took effect in Massachusetts; it eventually became the model for the federal legislation. More than fifty thousand children needing special education have already been blended into the Massachusetts school system. The majority have been steered into separate classrooms, but a good many have been absorbed in regular classes. Roughly eight million children nationwide — around twelve percent of the school-age population — are disabled. Prior to the passage of the Education for All Handicapped Children Act, only an estimated forty percent of them received sufficient special education. Under the law, all of them had to be shifted into the "least restrictive environment" by September 1978. The mission has been hazardous. Compliance has been lagging behind schedule. Nothing about this is cheap. Schools, already caught in a shrinking economy, figure they spend $2,800 a year to educate a handicapped child — double the cost of educating a normal student. In Charleston, South Carolina, a school spokesman calculated that the district paid from $2,300 to $5,000 annually to educate a disabled child, who must typically be placed in a smaller class and have special equipment. It spent $997.30 annually on the nonhandicapped Charleston student. The federal government, so far, will chip in only a small part of the handicapped pupil's bill. State officials figure that the government is bearing no more than about nine percent of the extra costs the schools are incurring. A total of $564 million was allocated in fiscal 1978, with the figure rising to $804 million in 1979.

Clearly, a brand-new classroom experience lies ahead for America's schoolchildren. Like many others of my generation, I moved through middle-class public schools without once encountering a child burdened with a handicap greater than the disinclination to study. No one who was disabled lived in the suburban town I grew up in. Mainstreaming promises to bring about a totally different student mix. Healthy children will still be in the majority, yes, but classes will also contain students who can't walk. Or see. Or hear. Or speak. Children who pant with the effort of getting a word out. Children who have to be carried from room to room. Children in respirators.

Some reports on mainstreaming sugarcoated early success stories: the stirring tale of the little blind girl who is, for the first time, brought into a normal classroom and, through a mixture of dogged determination and understanding classmates, quickly surmounts all obstacles. That, of course, is too simplistic. Heart-warming illustrations ignore the wide disparities of disabled children. Integrating one or two handicapped children is unarguably different from adding a sizable number of youngsters with myriad problems to the classroom of an ordinary, already harassed teacher. The difficulties are multiplied in direct proportion to the often inadequate preparation of the teachers and the equally skimpy facilities of the ordinary school.

Jim, seven, a victim of cerebral palsy, sat in a small wheel-chair, doing some reading. He looked forlorn. This was in Barbara Fagone's classroom. Robert, eight, who was emotionally disturbed, as were Marshall, six, and Patty, seven, were sprinkled elsewhere throughout the room of twenty-six students. (The names of the children have been changed.) All told, ninety-five students either physically disabled or suffering learning disabilities had taken their place in a school population of six hundred and eighty. Like the other teachers, Fagone had had no special instruction in coping with the handicapped.

Was the classroom much different with the disabled students? I asked her.

"It's fairly normal," Fagone said. "Handicapped kids are included in the recreation as much as possible. I mean, they can throw beanbags. They can do everything but run. It's just that when you call children up to the blackboard, the ones in wheelchairs and walkers take longer to get there. No one's impatient. No one shouts, 'Move it.' They get there."

What about failures? I asked.

She took no time to ponder her answer. "One girl transferred after two years here. She had a speech problem, a visual problem, and she was emotionally immature. She had spent three out of six years in a hospital. It was tough for her. We simply couldn't compensate. She went to another school with smaller classes. I just couldn't give her the individual attention she needed."

Fagone paused a moment, reflecting on what she had said, then added, "What we find is that mainstreaming is a very good idea, but you have to be careful. You can't just develop an individual program for every student. Not every student can make it. We're not the cure-all for everybody in the public schools. Not in a class of twenty-five students, that's for damn sure. This law sounds nice on paper, but after four years we see that it doesn't always work. Some students have to be segregated in special classrooms. Others belong here. If they are stuck in a hole somewhere, there's no way they could make it."

I roamed over to Peggy Hughey's classroom. She also taught first and second grades. Two of her students were severely handicapped. Both had cerebral palsy. One wore braces on her legs. Her name was Lois, and she was six. The other, nine-year-old Timmy, had much more serious motor problems. He suffered undetectable seizures that resulted in memory lapses, hunger, or loss of balance. He fell several times a day.

"You want to know how it is?" Hughey asked me. She had short red hair, big glasses, an intoxicating smile. "I think this school is good for one but not for another. Timmy has been in this school for four years and he hasn't progressed. He has stood still. He is still in first grade and he should be in third grade. We're asking that he be transferred to a special school for the handicapped. He doesn't remember his lessons. He can't write well. Sometimes he writes backwards. He can't remember where the bathroom is. Timmy falls off the chair and I have to dash over and pick him up. Taking care of the handicapped children is a big drain on my time. I have a lot of things on my mind. Lois, on the other hand, is fine. There's a vast difference between these two. So I can't just generalize and say all handicapped children should be mainstreamed."

I asked Hughey how comfortable she was working with handicapped children.

"I wasn't prepared for this," she said quietly. "I don't know when Timmy has seizures, and that scares the hell out of me. I am a regular elementary school teacher. I didn't choose the field of educating the handicapped. I don't mind Lois. I do mind Timmy. It is an awful burden on me. We are dancing around here on the lips of danger, and I don't want to be swallowed."

A pretty, trim, lithe brunette named Robin Clarke had been assigned to aid Hughey with Lois and Tina. She had the look of a cheerleader. She had been specially trained to work with handicapped children. The school has a total of four such aides. Explaining her role, Clarke said, "My mission is to give the handicapped kids extra help, the little additional boost they're likely to need to keep up with the regular students. But I don't spend time only with them. I spend time with all the kids in the class. That way the handicapped children aren't singled out and made to feel different. They don't realize I'm here just for them."

I inquired about Timmy.

Clarke's eyes shot around the room, and she cleared her throat. "It's clear he doesn't belong here anymore," she said. "Timmy right now, as you can see, is opening his book and he'll just sit there and stare at it, and he'll finally get frustrated and I'll have to help. But he'll forget what I tell him almost as soon as I tell him. We've talked with his mother, and she agrees that Timmy must go elsewhere."

The children were about to take a spelling test. It was a raucous classroom. The board and walls were crowded with primitive artwork and a list of class rules (don't go into anyone's desk but your own; no fighting; don't throw anything; listen to what your teacher says), though the rules didn't seem very well obeyed. One boy was bouncing a pencil against the wall. A girl wearing a T-shirt bearing the name "Gaucho" was taking crayons out of a Victor coffee can and cracking them apart, then dropping the pieces on the floor.

Two small boys were engaged in an aggressive wrestling bout near the door. Hughey, I felt, had her hands full keeping the turmoil from the able-bodied students within some bounds of control. I wondered how she could give any additional attention to handicapped students.

A student named Todd came over to me, and I asked him how he felt about the handicapped students in the room.

"We're all just kids here," he replied. "We're all alike, we all don't like school."

Timmy struggled over to where I was sitting. He held up his spelling book. "Am I doing this right?" he asked in slurred speech. "Am I doing this right?"

He wasn't.

Recess followed the spelling test, and while the students were out playing, Hughey said to me, "As you can see, I have one student who's a complete wacko. I have this other one who spends most of his time downstairs keeping the principal company. The discipline problems take every ounce out of me. So there's the thing when you bring in the handicapped children. Timmy needs a place without any distractions. Brother, this sure isn't it."

She paused to scream at a student who came barreling into the room. He barreled on out.

"You know, one of the other teachers has Lois for reading," she went on. "She gave her a C. Her mother came in here in a rage. She didn't want her daughter to be a *C* student; 'After all, can't you see she's handicapped?' The teacher told the mother that the school expects Lois to do normal work. If we were to tell the parents that we expected less of the handicapped children, the parents would yell, 'She *can* do as well!' So what approach are we supposed to take? We get our ears boxed either way."

Each handicapped student at the Trotter School spends a

portion of the school day in a special class in a "resource room." There, in small groups, they get additional instruction to help them keep pace with regular students. I went over to one of the resource rooms. A student in a wheelchair was there, along with five emotionally disturbed children, in the brightly lit and spacious room. Mary Ann Major, a big, plump woman and one of the resource teachers, told me that the kids come in for between a half-hour and an hour each day, depending on the severity of their needs. They return each week for another hour of art class.

Major said, "The idea is to have them practice to overcome their academic shortcomings in an environment where they won't be laughed at or stared at. That way they go back into the regular classroom and succeed. It's nice for them here. They're relaxed. They're away from the other children. So they always feel good about themselves in here."

How has it gone? I asked.

"From what I see, it's an excellent program. The work in here is at a level they can deal with and they don't get frustrated. In the regular classes, if they can't keep up they get angry and then they become discipline problems. The kids act totally different here from how they act in the normal classrooms. There's one who does nothing — absolutely zero, in his other classes. He does plenty in here. I have no doubt that before long he'll be doing plenty in all of his classes."

Next, I went downstairs to talk to John Bacci, who has been designated by the school to coordinate compliance with the law mandating equal education for everyone. He is moon-faced and apple-cheeked; his visage seemed to invite the outdoors into the room in which we sat. He said he was very busy, and he looked it. Papers, mostly having to do with handicapped students, were strewn about his office, and the phone rang as often as it does in a bookie's office around the time of a big race. I sat as he paced, seemingly propelled by an eagerness to move his thoughts.

Bacci told me that he spends most of his time sifting mounds of paper and meeting with parents and teachers to determine the proper placement for the students. "A team — parents, teachers, me — decide where a student is placed," Bacci said. "As a rule, everybody pretty much agrees as to what a child's needs are."

I said I was interested in the progress of the law.

"Nothing works a hundred percent," he said. "But things are getting better. Some areas have to be worked out. Teachers are losing a lot of time because of the meetings they have to attend. Teachers have to file quarterly reports on all the kids covered by the law. They have to arrange a yearly review in person with the parents. The paperwork is overwhelming, and a lot is redundant. Red tape. Waste of taxpayers' money. This legislation is picking up a lot of problems that aren't education problems. They're behavioral problems that we aren't equipped to deal with. We get kids whose problems are mostly with the parents, and the kids bring these problems to school with them. That isn't conducive to learning. They don't give a good goddamn about their arithmetic. It's like you or me coming to school with an awful stomachache. We're not interested in reading about Dick and Jane that day."

Continuing to pace restlessly, Bacci pointed a finger at a sheet of paper tacked to the wall. It outlined the major features of the state law. "That's the law," he said. "But that doesn't mean I have to agree with it. I don't agree with it. I'm all for mainstreaming. But we're getting the whole bag. I really am glad the special education classes are gone here. That's discrimination. You're telling a kid he's a dummy, he can't make it. I taught special education here, and every kid who came to my room knew he was different. Now, when they go only part of the day to a resource room, it's not so bad. But if a kid is beaten at home or doesn't get breakfast in the morning, what do we do? The strictly physically handicapped, as far as I'm concerned, are working out very nicely. Some can't make it, but most can. Parents have concerns, sometimes they're *too* concerned. The teachers generally adjust. But the kids with learning disabilities are something else again. I'm not sure they ought to be here."

No one knows just how mainstreaming should be accomplished. No one knows with any precision what commensurate special services ought to be provided — not in general, and not even in a particular situation. Two people of equal training will judge "adequacy" differently. One extreme is that lots of services must be available. The opposite extreme holds that regular teachers can handle whatever crops up, so special services are unnecessary. Dozens of slightly varying positions are taken along the bridge between these points of view. Subjective influences are obviously present. Someone who has devoted a career to perfecting methods of teaching the able-bodied tends to think disabled students require all manner of special assistance in the classroom. If one can imagine commensurate safeguards, one can also imagine veneer safeguards. Difficulties mount. Safeguards cost money. I have heard one knowledgeable educator say, "Teachers are scared out of their minds. Some of them are seriously wondering whether they should find a new profession. They are imagining the worst, nightmare situations. A cerebral palsy victim in one corner. A deaf student in the other. A blind student up front. A quadriplegic in the middle row. An epileptic near the window. Then they see every one of them having a problem all at the same time and all they can think of is bailing out."

I once asked a teacher who had never been exposed to a disabled student how difficult it would be for her to accustom herself to a mainstreamed classroom. She shrugged, smiled at some colleagues, and said, "There's the problem."

Frances Connor is chairman of the Special Education Department of Columbia University's Teachers College, based in New York. Her approach to the mainstreaming problem is, as she puts it, pragmatic, and she thinks that for many people it is, unfortunately, too much of an emotional issue. The effort, she thinks, is worth the candle. She thinks that the handicapped are too often "considered guilty until proven innocent." She believes that mainstreaming is here to stay, that reversion to segregation is impossible, and that schools — as a responsible unit of society, regulated by the government — will do the best they can. "What else can they do? Put handicapped children in a vault and turn the vault back to 1960?"

I had called on Connor at her sunny, plant-filled office well up on Manhattan's Upper West Side. An elegant, dark-haired woman in her forties, mildly formal in manner but without starch, in pants, a paisley blouse, light shoes, she spoke informally over interrupting phone calls. These were some of the things she said:

"I guess this is a dangerous statement, but I'm going to make it anyway. Some teachers frankly intend to circumvent the law. These teachers don't like the handicapped and they don't want to learn to like them.

"What are we trying to do — keep the standards of the classroom from falling off, or acclimate people to the handicapped? The mainstreaming problem is out of focus.

"I can't believe that the problems will be of such magnitude that they'll be unmanageable.

"Mainstreaming is frustrating. The process is difficult to get a good handle on. I'm very concerned about the end result of all this.

"If I were calling the shots, I would have given three years for compliance. Many school districts aren't ready now. Some of them don't want to be ready. What I fear is people inventing creative ways of getting around the law.

"I know that teachers will have to undergo retraining. What upsets me more than anything else is the attitude of some of the teachers toward the children they're going to get. A teacher I was talking with recently referred to a mildly retarded student, a child we would think of as marvelously competent, as a vegetable. It sickens me."

Connor talked about the controversial element of the legislation that requires schools to draft individual education plans for handicapped pupils. "The hope is that this will stimulate a productive involvement of parents in the educational system. But one fear I have is that teachers will underestimate rather than set the goals of a student high enough. They won't want to take the risk that the child can't cut the mustard, leaving them open for blame."

Since support services will take a while to develop in many classrooms, Connor said she expects some parental backlash during the early stages of mainstreaming. "Many regular students are going to be held back by the handicapped students in their classes. So the parents of these children are going to be angry. Some parents of college-bound students are already threatening countersuits."

What about the handicapped students? I asked.

Connor said, "I think one-third of the students who are mainstreamed will do better than anyone could have imagined. They'll absolutely blossom. Another one-third will hold their own. And I daresay about a third, without the proper support systems, will be in desperate trouble."

* * *

The federal Office for Civil Rights has already accused the New York City school system, largest in the nation, of illegally discriminating against some handicapped children by permitting lengthy waiting lists for evaluation and placement. It has complained that New York has been allowing disabled students a shorter school day, rather than having them keep pace with the other students. The board of education has denied the charges, though it confesses that it has been overwhelmed by the federal law. It had its own accountants, Touche Ross & Company, study the problem, and the result was a stinging report that discovered nine thousand empty seats for handicapped children in the system, about six hundred and fifty classes' worth, enough to wipe out the entire waiting list. The report, which was issued in March 1978, further found that to place a single pupil in a special education class was requiring seven to eight months on average, almost a school year. The law mandates placement within sixty days. It takes even longer, the report found, to transfer a handicapped child from the special education program to a regular classroom. Seven separate administrative steps were involved. An estimated $33 million in teacher costs were being wasted annually on empty seats in classrooms. In New York, the cost of educating a severely handicapped child in the public schools was put at about $7,100, compared with $2,400 for an able-bodied student. Responding to the study, Ronald Walter, deputy chancellor of schools, said, "The expansion of special education, the complexity of the law and the problems of staffing and expensive financing for handicapped children happened over a very short period of time. It has been tougher than we imagined. It has been much tougher." The Touche Ross study recommended a massive reorganization of the Division of Special Education and Pupil Personnel Services; Walter has agreed to it.

* * *

The TV camera pans over a muscular young man with raveled hair. He starts to speak. Clearly, the effort is painful. "They told my parents I'd never live past three," he says. His face is wrinkled from the struggle to form words. "But here I am." He pauses to rouse the energy to go on. "They told my parents that I'd never talk, but I talked at five. They said I'd never be able to drive, but after nine years of training my body" — he pauses, pants — "I can drive a car." He grins, triumphant that he has said what he had to say. "And now I'm getting married in three months." Jimmy is his name. He suffers from cerebral palsy.

Suzanne, a bright sixteen-year-old deaf girl is observed as she fumbles with test tubes in a chemistry lab. Next, she learns to rappel on a tree in an outdoor class. Her speech is so slow and garbled that it must be dubbed on the screen. Lisa, a severely retarded eighteen-year-old with multiple handicaps, is eating with a spoon. Getting the hang of it was tantamount to an able-bodied person learning to assemble an engine.

They were a few of the subjects of "Including Me," a TV special shown on Public Broadcasting stations and some commercial channels. The government has used the film, along with magazine ads featuring some of the children, to introduce the public to mainstreaming in the schools and to explain the Education for All Handicapped Children Act. During the show, you hear the voices of parents who despair that their children will ever get a proper public education. Suitably enough, the narrator is Patricia Neal. She had herself recovered, miraculously, from a brutal stroke. The show ends with a plea to see that the federal act is properly implemented. The public is urged to talk to PTAs, talk to principals, talk to school boards, talk to their children.

Elsewhere, other approaches are being tried. The Easter

Seal Society furnishes handicapped lecturers who will travel to schools to discuss disability. The organization feels an obligation to prepare society for the handicapped. Also, it shrewdly came up with the scheme of equipping schools with "disability kits" comprised of blindfolds, wheelchairs, leg braces, and braille reading matter. Before disabled students are brought into classrooms, teachers have the normal children attempt to read Braille. They eat while blindfolded. They swoop along in wheelchairs. They watch soundless TV. Five Rhode Island schools have already experimented with the program and found that children get into it with a flurry of energy. "The laws are catapulting these handicapped kids into the classroom so fast that it can be a rude awakening for the regular kids if they're not prepared," an Easter Seal person told me. "This program makes the normal children temporarily disabled. It's an eye-opening experience. They understand what it's like to have limitations. I've had some adults give it a crack, and they're amazed. Get into a wheelchair for a day sometime and see how helpless you suddenly find yourself."

Inequity is still latent in the legislation. Day-care centers and preschool education have been shortchanged by the federal and state laws enacted so far. Some doubt this is the best place to start, on grounds that kids at this age are generally socially immature. But what better time to expose them to new things? I talked to Helene Ginsberg, a polite woman with a ready sense of mirth, who is an adviser at the Institute for Family and Child Study in East Lansing, Michigan. The institute coordinates training programs for children under five years old. Because of protracted pressure by the parents of disabled children, the organization has been mainstreaming handicapped children into the two day-care centers, two nursery schools, and two parental cooperatives it oversees. Already about twenty-five disabled kids have been moved in among the five hundred and fifty normal children.

"It's been going fantastically," Ginsberg told me. "The kids are between a year and a year-and-a-half, and we see a lot of positive interaction. A number of handicapped and nonhandicapped children have developed an abiding liking for each other. We see that the kids become aware of the differences of their classmates without placing any negative connotations on them. In some cases, in fact, the handicapped student acquires the higher status. One child, for instance, has a very serious seizure disorder. He wears a helmet to protect himself. We thought he would really be made fun of with this helmet on. As it turned out, many of the kids went home and requested helmets so they could look just like him. They thought he looked neat. I was in the class the other day and saw another child with him; they both had on those little red helmets."

7

At Michigan State University, a sprawling hodgepodge of buildings, sports arenas, theaters, and swimming pools, the students — mostly jeans-clad and barefoot — were finishing with their finals and packing their duffel bags for the summer recess. A half-dozen undergraduates were lounging near the stunted shrubs outside the library or on the grass. One held a Frisbee. An air conditioner was rattling in a window. Nice out here. The Office of Programs for Handicappers was on the fourth floor of the library, reachable by elevator. Stapled to a bulletin board in the hallway were two large black-and-white posters. One of them read, "This Land Was Made For You And Me." It depicted a bearded dwarf shoving a bigger man in a wheelchair across a grassy field. The man in the chair was clutching an American flag. The other poster said, "Let's Be More Than Friends." It pictured a young, attractive woman cuddled up seductively in a chaise lounge. She was wearing a bathrobe. A folded wheelchair was beside her.

"Welcome to the hot spot," Judy Taylor called out from inside the office. A slight woman in her thirties, with a rich thatch of wavy brown hair, she had on an ill-fitting print dress. She is intelligent, and her directness suggests honesty and candor. Polio put her in a wheelchair when she was eight. Her arms are withered and are mounted on swivel braces on her motorized chair. The setup gives her the look of a marionette.

In 1965, Judy Taylor was the first wheelchair user to enroll at Michigan State, which had some forty thousand students who didn't need wheelchairs. Friends strongly advised her to go elsewhere, but Judy had a stubborn streak and didn't listen to them. She grew up in Lansing, Michigan, near the Michigan State campus, and she sensibly chose to go there. The medical director subjected her to a "survival" test — and flunked her. However, the admissions people at the school were supportive, and she was allowed in. She didn't then own an electric wheelchair, but her mother did a lot of huffing and puffing, and two sororities took on, as a project, responsibility for pushing her around the East Lansing campus. "It worked erratically. I got stranded a lot." She picked her major with an eye to which classes she could get to. Journalism intrigued her, but to this day the journalism school isn't accessible to wheelchairs. She took up fine arts. "It was kind of lonely out there, being the only wheelchair on campus. I was like the only weed in a bed of roses. But I learned to enjoy my own company." Outspoken by nature, Taylor planted the seeds of student activism and, along with another student wheelchair user, Eric Gentile, she fought hard to get the school to make its enormous campus accessible to the disabled.

In time, school administrators caved in. They agreed to undertake an ambitious Project Access that attacks all the fundamental obstacles to the handicapped. According to the plan, the school would spend between three million and five million dollars over a period of fifteen to seventeen years to make the jumble of 386 buildings available to all. Split into ten phases, the plan was begun in April 1974. No other program at any other college in the country quite approaches the Michigan State project. Publicity about it has wooed a substantial stream of disabled students to the school. Thirty wheelchair users now clack around campus, and a total of nearly five hundred handicapped students, most of them blind, have enrolled.

Mainstreaming the handicapped into colleges has become one of the most controversial, incendiary issues that higher education has faced in recent years. Most colleges view mainstreaming in terms of money, and they fear that they stand to pay the steepest price of all. By mid-1980, their halls must be accessible to the handicapped. Barriers to mobility must be done away with. Admission tests must be adjusted if they discriminate against disabilities — such as lack of motor skills — that don't affect academic ability. Counselors must not steer handicapped students away from curriculum choices because of preconceptions about their capabilities. Auxiliary aids — tapes for the blind, interpreters for the deaf, and various basic contrivances such as jacks for tape recorders — must be available. No definite figures are available on how many colleges have already made extensive efforts to stamp out physical barriers and furnish support services for disabled students and employees, but indications are that only a few have. The result has been a storm of protest. The American Council on Education has said that response to the Rehabilitation Act has been "as large" and as "spontaneous" as on any piece of legislation having to do with higher education. The council reckons that if all institutions have to make themselves entirely accessible to all kinds of handicapped people, the price tag will amount to a staggering $4.5 billion.

No one really knows much about the handicapped in education — their needs, their numbers, the degree and kinds of discrimination they have suffered. The important question, for now unanswerable, is how many will turn up to take advantage of the new law. The National Association of Independent Colleges and Universities has protested that the cost of compliance for the sake of a few, will drive up tuition for all students. Immense state schools like the University of Missouri, which calculates the outlay for structural changes on its four campuses at $10 million, are banging on the doors of state legislatures. College administrators aren't happy. They say they are put in the position of having to beg money, like monks seeking alms. Many educators seem to take the entire prospect with a grain of doubt. Remarks by, for example, school administrators, education observers, and teachers go like this:

"Who can figure out what 'reasonable accommodations' and 'undue hardships' mean? We are at our wit's end deciding what to do."

"HEW writes hundreds of pages of regulations in very fine print. The question is: How in the world can you realistically implement them?"

"We are a small school. We have old buildings and irregular topography. The law spells financial ruin for us."

"We are a small school, and soon we will be no school."

"What we have here is a very punitive approach toward higher education. This is a terrible step backward, because it puts the handicapped in an adversary position to the universities."

"This could bankrupt schools. It means diverting scarce academic resources into more administrative work."

"The regulations are a grotesque intrusion on internal campus governance in the name of principles which have not been defined clearly enough to be administered. If you want to take things to their extreme, HEW could move in on a university that refuses to allow a person who is tone deaf to major in music. What contribution do you think that person will make to the field of music?"

HEW has been trying to be lenient. It has agreed that, well, water fountains don't have to be lowered for wheelchair users; put a paper-cup dispenser nearby. Elevators don't have to be installed everywhere; move a class to the first floor. Not all living quarters and bathrooms have to be modified, just a representative sample. Mistakes have been made. The University of Texas installed an elevator for wheelchairs in the student union at a cost of $17,000. Then it discovered that the elevator was too tiny for a passenger in a wheelchair plus an attendant.

Nelda Barnes has been deaf since she was six. In the summer of 1977, she enrolled at Converse College, a private liberal arts school in Spartanburg, South Carolina, to pick up some extra credits. She asked Converse to supply her with a sign-language interpreter. The college said no. Barnes took Converse to court. In the first court test of HEW's regulations, a district court judge ruled in her favor: although Barnes paid just $210 in tuition, Converse must pay eight dollars an hour — $750 by the end of the summer session — for a sign-language specialist. "What Congress is doing," retorted Converse president Robert Coleman, "is appropriating private funds for what it deems a public good."

The biggest impact of the law, however, is not expected to be felt till fifteen to twenty years from now. After all, many children with handicaps haven't yet gotten the kind of elementary and secondary school education that qualifies them for college. Nevertheless, a few colleges have long been struggling to make their campuses accessible without visible qualms, even while disagreeing about how to attack the problem. The University of Illinois at Champaign-Urbana began making changes years ago to accommodate the flow of disabled World War II veterans. A separate office deals with the handicapped, and the campus provides a special bus service, appropriately equipped first-floor living quarters, and building entrance ramps. Shower seats have been put in for wheelchair users and spigots have wide blades for those who can't grasp handles. All campus signs include braille translations. A team of five hundred and fifty volunteers tape lectures, make braille transcriptions, and learn sign language so that they can assist deaf students in class. An average of two hundred disabled students enroll at the school every year.

But many handicapped people find the Illinois system unpalatable. They think the approach is custodial, worse than nothing at all. The handicapped resent being forced to fill out special forms made up of irrelevant questions. They think special housing for the disabled is segregationalist, that a place like the University of Illinois makes things so easy for disabled students that they don't have to bother to develop their own resourcefulness. How, they ask, will they be able to move toward independent lives when they get out of school? Instead, they find more luring the kind of work going on at Michigan State.

I flew to East Lansing one fresh, sunny day so that Judy Taylor and Eric Gentile could show me the campus and tell me about their ideas on accessibility. We started off with lunch at the State Room in Kellog Hall, a popular meeting-place for local conventions. Taylor had trouble getting comfortable at the table we were given. There wasn't much space between our table and the next one. A man seated at the adjacent table gaped at her peevishly. She ignored him.

"That's his problem if there's not enough room between

tables," Gentile snapped. "Why should we excuse ourselves? We can't condense our wheelchairs."

"Right on," Taylor smiled.

Gentile is a big, fair-skinned man. Sandy hair. In his thirties. Often a bemused smile. His voice is smoothly rolling and timpanic. Gentile is, by his description, a "foaming-at-the-mouth radical. I tend to scream and shout and beat my head against the walls." When Gentile was twenty-two, he was coming home from work on his motorcycle (this was in Detroit, and he was working at a tool and die plant), when he fell asleep. He missed a curve and plowed head-on into a tree. "The tree didn't give. My spinal cord did." He has sat in a wheelchair ever since. He has powerful arm muscles and the agility to perform the arduous, frightening art of transferring out of his chair into a regular seat. He tools around campus in a car equipped with hand controls.

Since becoming handicapped, Gentile has studied and became proficient at architecture and was the mastermind behind Project Access. I asked him to identify the principles of the project.

He answered, "We're rejecting the medical model of disability. We're opposed to barrier-free design and believe in environmental design. Barrier-free design embraces mostly special programs and segregation. Special this. Special that. Special everything. We're dedicated to mainstreaming. Here, auxiliary aids aren't foisted on anyone. They are supplied only on request. The physical remaking of the campus is done in such a way that the handicappers don't use special entrances and aren't relegated to particular housing. Instead of ramps, which I happen to think are pretty ugly, all buildings possible are being done with railing-free grade-level entrances that everyone uses. They also happen to be easier to plow in winter. We get snow here by the mountain.

Randomly selected dorm rooms are done over so that handicappers can live with everyone else. You don't have to do much — put in tubs instead of showers, widen doors, have levers instead of doorknobs. If you use your head, it's not a big deal."

Gentile hiked his glasses higher on his wide nose, crossed his arms and stared out the window at the campus as though he were uneasy and wary of it.

"The idea is to set up a model of a campus in which environmental quality has been maximized for handicappers," he said. "We're doing more with what you can do once you get into a building than merely making the bathroom available. We're not here to mother anybody. We're here to provide equality in education."

Neither "disabled" nor "handicapped" is part of Gentile's or Taylor's vocabulary. They refer to anybody who's disabled as a handicapper. Gentile explained, "We regard the word 'disabled' the same way blacks look on the word 'nigger.' If you look up the definition of 'handicapper,' you find it means someone who rates odds for success. Someone who is stigmatized by society has the right to judge how that stigma will affect his life, not society. So that person is the handicapper. We have been stigmatized by society, and we are all handicappers."

The first phase of the Michigan State project provided access to the principal public buildings. Only in extreme cases were ramps used. During subsequent phases, paths wide enough for wheelchairs will be strung across campus. One of the four campus swimming pools will be modified with a ramp. Space for wheelchairs will be cleared in the football stadium. Elevator control panels will be lowered from forty-eight to thirty-six inches. Equipment in science laboratories will be redesigned or remodeled to include, among other things, adjustable desks that can be lowered or raised. Buses accessible to the handicapped will be shuttling around the campus.

"I feel a sense of optimism," Taylor said. "We're building, but the down payment is a great deal of sacrifice, a lot of work that has to be put in. People talk about how they are going to win the lottery. We have that sense of the future, of good things ahead."

Taylor is a spunky individual. She has not let her paralysis inhibit her. She has become interested in target shooting. She has had a .357 Magnum mounted onto a board that attaches to her wheelchair, and she rumbles out to the range ("I look like a rolling cannon") and fires away. She likes to ice-skate. She takes her chair onto the ice and slips and slides. "You can sort of control where you're going. At least I haven't toppled over yet." The school administration was distraught at the prospect of wheelchairs on the ice, and attempted to ban the idea. The handicapped students protested. So they were allowed to "skate" as long as a second person accompanied them. The rules neglected, however, to specify that the second person be able-bodied, and pairs of wheelchair users now careen around on the ice.

I asked Taylor how good a job she thought most colleges were doing in complying with the federal regulations.

"Not a good job at all," she replied. "It's the deadline that's a killer. You can't do quality work in the time frame they're allowing. The deadline is the same for a community college as it is for a place this big. A university like this one can't take that deadline seriously."

Gentile said, "There are three hundred and eighty-six buildings here and five thousand acres. What do you do with this place? So the federal regulations come out and say rebuild the place by 1980, and you look at them. And they're not giving us any bucks."

"Under the rules," Taylor said, "each school has to put

down on paper a transition plan indicating what changes will be made, and on what schedule the changes will occur. Some university administrators are putting down only what they think can be accomplished. It's not just that the deadline is too short. The regulations don't make *total* accessibility a requirement in the long run. The way it is now, HEW is only going to do spot checks and respond to specific complaints from students. So the system, to work, depends upon activist handicappers. And many places don't have any. I fear that most colleges will do the minimum and go about their business as usual."

When Michigan State started on its project, the federal government provided about eighty percent of the initial $400,000 outlay. The school put up the balance. Since then, however, the university hasn't been able to attract any further federal dollars. Taylor said, "We met with our congressman a few days ago, and he said the mood of Congress is such that they'll wait a year before approving any barrier-removal funds. First they'll see how the other possibilities, like rescheduling of classes, work out."

I asked Taylor how many schools she thought would be accessible in their entirety by 1980.

"None," she said.

Done with lunch, we left Kellog Hall and filed into Taylor's van. It sported hand controls that enabled Gentile to drive. We set out to take a tour of the campus. Once we were comfortably settled in the van, Taylor discovered that her battery had almost run down. She said she would return to the office and get charged up while Gentile and I looked over the school.

The sun was brilliant, and the sky above the campus, all the way to the horizon, was banded with ribs of cirrus clouds. The air was clean and smelled pleasantly like laundry bleach. As we pulled out of the parking lot beside Kellog Hall, Gentile spotted a metal wheelchair accessibility sign that had been bent out of shape. He shook his head in disgust. "Why don't those bastards grow up before they get here," he said.

The campus is an arresting sight. The facilities are impeccable. A tall brick student center rises like a battlement at one end. Stately buildings, ivy crawling up some of them, dominate the central chunk of the layout. There are three outdoor swimming pools and one indoor pool. Outdoor and indoor tennis courts. A golf course. An indoor baseball field. A new arena for ice hockey and ice shows and an occasional religious revival meeting. A section of housing for undergraduates, one for graduate students and one for married students. To get through the campus maze, you need a car. Buses are a substitute.

As we drove along, Gentile said, "When a handicapper goes to college, it's like a stranger visiting a revered person's home. He sits narrowly on the couch, like an uncertain guest. Colleges should be as much our home as anyone else's."

We shuddered to a stop in front of one of the classroom buildings, a towering brick affair. A dog lay in front of the building, flattened out into a curly mass, unmoving, like a rug spread on the grass to dry. "That's the Natural Sciences Hall," Gentile said. "Steps used to be there. Now, as you can see, there's a grade-level entrance that you'd never know hadn't been there from day one." That was true. The front had been redone in weathered brick that matched the brick of the original building. "The thing cost sixteen grand. The job was cancelled on me three times. It takes a lot of head-knocking. One thing I didn't get was a snow-melting system under the sidewalk. It would have cost another ten thousand, but from a handicapper's standpoint it's surely worth it. We don't have snowplows attached to our wheelchairs. Snow is a real nemesis for us."

Moving deeper into the campus, Gentile said, "We're very very much in favor of phasing things in. That way you don't place too much of a demand on society all at once, and you have a chance to do a quality job. We're big on quality here."

As the van bounded along, Gentile pointed out a spot along the road to my right. "There's a place where we raised the road to reach the sidewalk, rather than lower the sidewalk to meet the road. Cheaper and faster that way."

We took a look at the High Energy Physics Lab, where a concrete ramp had been put in alongside some steps. "We'll take it, but if *I* had my druthers I'd have used grade level. But I didn't have control of the budget on that one."

Down the road, we came to the Kresge Art Gallery. "Oh, look at this thing," Gentile said. He threw his head back and laughed. "I can't wait to get my bite into this one." Two flights of stairs, one with four steps and the other with seven, led to the building. "I'd like a gradually increasing grade-level entrance with no steps. All somebody has to do is say they've got the bucks and I'll get going."

We parked on another street and gazed at the chemistry building. "Look at that," Gentile groaned. His hair flew in the wind. "That's what they built before I got into this." To the left of the stairs fronting the building was a very steep ramp beside a two-foot drop-off into a rock garden. "Try getting up that with a wheelchair," Gentile said. "With a rocket-powered chair, you've got a shot at it. A blind student came out of that entrance, slipped and broke his ankle. That kind of access does nothing but increase the population of disabled students."

Gentile fired up the van and we puttered on. He said, "If

you ask the faculty if some of these buildings are accessible, they'll say, 'Oh yeah, oh yeah. Sure they are. Why, I saw a wheelchair user being carried up the stairs just yesterday.' " We flickered past another classroom building that allowed access only through a garage. Gentile said, "I have this nasty habit of thinking of handicappers as people, not as freight. So I don't call that accessible. I call that repulsive."

The brand-new Clinical Science Center had no stairs and no ramps anywhere. Everything was grade level. "Why is that?" Gentile asked. "That's because I got to the university architect ahead of time and told him that it wouldn't cost a cent more to make everything grade level and so how about it? Sure, he said. When you have time, it can be a cinch to make places accessible."

We moved on, and Gentile remembered a more disconcerting incident. "We had this one classroom building where all these handicappers found themselves stranded outside in the snow, unable to get in. I came up with a set of proposals to solve the problem. I presented them to the university engineer. He ranted and raged, and then he leaned back in his chair and said, 'Now, Eric, don't you think that the real solution to this problem is to have these people move South?' Ever since then, we have been deadly enemies."

We passed a parking lot adjacent to a dormitory. Gentile screeched to a stop. "Now look at that," he said. "We don't want that." A ramp led from the parking lot to the sidewalk. A No Parking sign poked up next to it. "That creates attitudinal problems," he said. "People hate No Parking signs to begin with. When they see that ramp, they realize that the sign is there so handicappers can get onto the sidewalk. So they direct hostility against handicappers. It's a bad deal all around."

Next, we visited the married housing complex, which, unbelievably, was situated on Cherry Lane. One batch of apartments had steps outside. Another cluster that Gentile had worked on sported flat entrances. As we tooled through the compound, Gentile spotted some ramps leading from the sidewalk to the road. They were clearly too narrow for a normal-sized wheelchair, and therefore wholly unusable. "Jesus," Gentile said. He batted his fist against his head. "If you're not on these workmen all the time, you don't get the job done right. Pitiful. Just pitiful. I have to crack the whip constantly."

We arrived at Albert and Sarah Case hall, an undergraduate dorm. Gentile slipped the van into a parking spot, and we moseyed inside to look at a modified room. Students were loading up cars and moving out. The semester had just ended. "I'm free, I'm free," a bushy-haired student was shouting to no one in particular. The hallway was littered with debris — beer bottles, corkboard, paper bags, discarded record jackets.

We ambled down a section marked "Extremity Street." A sign on the wall said, "Wanted dead or alive (preferably alive). We need (desperately!) male volunteers to act as wheelchair attendants for a muscular dystrophy camp." We entered a room in the middle of the hall. The bathroom had been enlarged into a giant room, with a tub that had support railings. Railings were alongside the toilet, as well. The doorway was wider than normal, with lever handles. The rod in the clothes closet had been lowered so that clothes could be hung up from a sitting position. A remote-control lightswitch was mounted on the desk. "You have to do a lot to new dorm rooms," Gentile said. "They build them as tight as they can. Save the dough is the operative phrase. So you've got to knock down walls, because handicappers are much more horizontal people."

As we emerged from the room, we bumped into a student

coming down the hall in a wheelchair. He had a Frisbee in his lap. He gave out a wide grin.

"How goes it?" Gentile asked.

"Ah, it could be worse," the student said.

Gentile introduced me to the student, a sophomore majoring in English. I asked him how he found the treatment in the dorm.

"I am treated exactly like everyone else," he replied. "I am regarded as a lunatic."

We took a quick peek at the immense football stadium, scene of some of the great moments in college football history. Two undergraduates were whacking tennis balls against one of the outer stadium walls. There was only one elevator, intended to whisk reporters and photographers up to the press box. No space at that level was available for anybody in a wheelchair, so handicapped students who showed up were directed down onto the playing field, where the view was generally lousy. Gentile said he hoped to get space reserved for wheelchairs near the press box.

Finally, we rumbled over to one of the vast gymnasiums. Gentile pointed out that some shower controls had been lowered so a seated person could operate them. Then we ventured outside and looked at one of the Olympic-sized pools. Clumps of students were taking the sun on the neatly trimmed grass encircling the pool, others were splashing around in the water. No sign of anyone disabled. Gentile sat off to one side and, in a professorial tone of voice, described the pool as "a big waste of space right now as far as handicappers are concerned." It was something the disabled deserved to have access to, that seemed to be his message. He said that he had tried to coax the former director of athletics into making the pool available to the handicapped by putting in a ramp. "He gave us a hard time, and nothing happened. We tried to tell him that you've got to look at these changes as insurance, because almost everybody's going to be a handicapper some day. Still no luck. His head was like a rock. Six months later, as poetic justice I guess, he had a stroke and is now in a wheelchair himself. His doctor told him that swimming would be extremely beneficial to him. He retired, however. The pool, as you can see, still isn't accessible."

8

A STEAMING hot day on Roosevelt Island. The air was smoky with summertime. The sun shone down with a vengeance on the twisting, European-style Main Street. Not a car was in sight, only the minibus, which is free. Starlings were having some sort of meeting in the park. Mothers wheeling baby strollers ambled past. A game of handball was in progress against a wall. "C'mon, Jack, hit that damn ball," a pasty boy said with some disgust. "What d'you think you got hands for?" "Ah, Bob, why don't you swallow the ball." Milling about the arcade across from one of the apartment houses was a group of quadriplegics in their electric wheelchairs, chatting amiably. The weather, prices at the Sloan's down the block, social plans seemed to be the topics. Across the street, another quadriplegic trundled by, moving with the same feckless insouciance as the ten-year-olds who swooped by on skateboards. He seemed in a hurry, as if late for a movie. A fish-shaped finger of land floating on the threshold of Manhattan, the riverbound, two-and-a-half-mile-by-eight-hundred-foot complex was conceived in 1969 as a mixed-income, racially balanced new community. Patients from two chronic hospitals located there — Coler and Goldwater — are often on the streets and in the stores. And among the roughly five thousand residents are fifty-six wheelchair users leading independent lives, one of the most visible concentrations of severely disabled people in any community in the country. For one of the founding principles of Roosevelt Island was that it be totally accessible to the handicapped.

I had taken the bright red aerial tram from Manhattan one day to see what life was like for the disabled on the island. The gondola rocked gently in the wind. When I got across, I caught the first minibus downtown. The bus was equipped with an extra-wide door, and a ramp shot out from underneath to allow a wheelchair to rattle aboard. As it happened, no wheelchairs were on my particular bus, just a couple of kids in their early teens and an elderly couple with a Bloomingdale's bag. The bus clacked past Goldwater Hospital — a hulking, imposing structure — then rolled through bucolic countryside and finally swept into town. I got off at one of the first of the half-dozen apartment houses on the island, and dropped in on Ira and Vicki Holland.

Braille markings protruded from the elevator panel, and the buttons were set low enough so that a person sitting in a wheelchair could easily reach them. The hallways were uncommonly wide. One of the Hollands' attendants answered the door and motioned me in. Propped up in their electric wheelchairs, Ira and Vicki shouted their greetings from the living room. "Drink?" Ira said as I came in. "We've got beer, juice, soft drinks, even some hard stuff, if that's your pleasure." I asked for a beer and the attendant hurried off to fetch it.

Ira is thirty-nine, with a chunky face and thinning hair. A miniature beard tufts from the point of his chin. Deep-set, lively eyes peer at the world with stubborn distrust. Even sitting in a wheelchair, Ira seemed in motion, about to leap up to do a job, to wrench the world to the shape his hands desired. Vicki is forty-three, with short, wavy black hair, merry eyes, and a soft voice. Ira is far the more talkative of the two. Both are quadriplegics, polio victims who, until a year ago, lived in Goldwater Hospital. They met and married there. Their courtship lasted four years ("We wanted to be sure"), then they married in 1968. During most of their lives they had never thought of setting up a life outside the hospital. But others moved out and liked it. They talked it over between themselves. The hospital was safe and all, but why not move out? Hospitals are for sick people, and we're not sick. Why not try a new life? Why not? Why not? Can we afford to, Ira? I think so, Vicki. Let's do it. Okay, let's do it.

The tidy two-bedroom apartment was tastefully furnished in modern style. In the living room stood a six-foot-high rack with dozens of magazines and books. In casual piles, books littered windowsills and tables and spilled a trail into the main bedroom adjacent. A forest of plants stood in one corner of the bedroom, and a door debouched onto a balcony that looked out to a downward-sloping lawn and pleasant shade trees. As I went through the rooms, I was struck by the absence of any trace of alterations to allow for the fact that the tenants were two severely handicapped people. Before I could mention this, Ira piped up, "You may notice that this apartment is as normal as one you might rent. And we haven't any gizmos hidden in the closets or anything. Nothing descends out of the ceiling. This happens to be a standard two-bedroom apartment designed for people who are perfectly fit. What are we doing in it? Well, some special apartments here have railings in the bathroom, wide showers, low counters, and so forth. Those are no good at all for us. We need an attendant all the time anyway. We're not going to be taking showers. We're not going to be cooking. So when we decided to move out of the hospital, we said, Hey, don't put us in any modified apartment. We'll take the standard place. We have to think of what's going to work well for our attendants. They're doing the housework."

As I sat down to sip my beer, Ira said to me, "All of this is a lot of what the handicapped-rights movement is after. We would like the entire country to be something like Roosevelt Island. A place where we can get about, and where we are treated like anybody else. Like everyone on earth, we just want to live our own lives. We want to be part of the community."

"You know, in the rest of New York you go out of your apartment and you can only go a square block and that's it," Vicki said. "We can get to any part of this island. We weren't unhappy in the hospital, you realize. We could have stayed there forever and not gone out of our minds. But we had long outgrown our need for the hospital. We no longer had any business being there. This is where we belong."

Ira screwed his face into a prune, and went into a long harangue against bureaucrats. "The whole problem is with the bureaucrats," he said. "They think we need a big brother. Let us live our lives as best we can. We seem to do a pretty good job of it when we're given the chance. We know what we need. Nobody else does. We're not animals. We don't have to be told what's good for us, what's not good for us. We have to be physically helped in certain ways, sure. But our minds are as sharp as anyone else's. We know what we want, dammit!"

Both Ira and Vicki got college degrees when they were at Goldwater. Each holds a B.A. in psychology, although regular jobs for them are hardly feasible. Being as severely disabled as they are, they must have attendant care around the clock. They need electric wheelchairs as well as respirators (neither can breathe on his or her own); Ira has a type of respirator that wraps around his chest and aids his breathing,

Vicki needs a rocking bed (fourteen rocks per minute) that helps her breathe. Both need hydraulic lifts to get in and out of bed. Their medical care is very expensive. They must go to Goldwater for monthly checkups, and their equipment requires frequent and costly maintenance and replacement. (To furnish their apartment, they sold Fuller Brush and Amway products to hospital employees for two years. "It was a real buster," Ira will say. "I've come to hate those products. You can sing someone's praises only so long before what you loved you begin to detest.") At the moment, they receive Supplemental Security Income payments, food stamps, Medicaid coverage, and a housing subsidy. If they worked, these benefits would probably end and they'd have to pay their gigantic bills themselves. One day Ira calculated that Vicki and he, leading an uncommonly thrifty existence, amass more than $60,000 in annual expenses.

"No way we could crack that nut," he said. "I wasn't planning on getting hired as the president of General Motors first thing. So the system, you see, provides an incentive not to work. Worse, the handicapped are actually punished for working."

Vicki and Ira lived at Goldwater at a cost of $210 a day each, or $12,600 a month for the two of them. "So wouldn't you as a taxpayer rather have us living here in our own apartment?" Ira said. "It's a lot easier on the wallet."

Ira sipped some of his drink through a straw. He furrowed his brow. He said, "Vicki and I are militants. Not everyone else is. Disability doesn't make you something different, except you're not walking around. You're still the same person. If we weren't disabled, we'd probably be militant about some other issue that hit close to home."

Ira pointed out the hassles of getting their equipment fixed. "You need experienced people to take care of chairs and respirators. You can't take these things to your local garage. Goldwater used to repair them and get reimbursed by Medicaid. Yet they weren't always reimbursed. Now they have a very limited repair service. Lifecare, in Boulder, Colorado, has a monopoly on the respirator market. Royal Carpenter, in Queens, is their New York representative. Lifecare won't service anyone on Medicaid. They will service people on Medicare — people who are over sixty-two or have worked enough years to qualify. Lots of places don't want to deal with New York Medicaid. They have to put up with long waiting periods for payments, sloppy handling, poor administration. Seven respiratory patients live in this complex. About a hundred live in and around New York. Goldwater is the only hospital between here and California that has a respiratory center. Now who in the hell are we supposed to go to? Goldwater says, 'We'll do it but somebody better pay us.' Lifecare says, 'We have no contract with Medicaid.' Goldwater is reimbursed only for inpatients, not outpatients like us. On the average, we need monthly work done. So far, Goldwater has obliged us free of charge. I think it's a damn shame Medicaid doesn't get its act together before we stop breathing."

Equally troublesome for them is the matter of attendants. Ira and Vicki employ three people who work shifts to provide twenty-four-hour coverage. To find them, the Hollands placed newspaper ads and interviewed over a hundred respondents. "This city is crawling with people who are willing to do this kind of work," Ira said. "After all, a lot of unemployed people are drifting about. But we didn't want any ordinary Joe working in our home. These people are extensions of our lives. In fact, they turn our respirators on and off. So our lives are in their hands."

Vicki said, "We were looking for somebody who was willing to learn. We were looking for someone who was flexible and who was willing to commit himself to living with us, not just working for us. We could have hired people with lots of training. Registered nurses, for instance. We didn't want that. We wanted self-determination, and people flexible to roll with us. We finally narrowed our selection down to three people. Prior to these jobs, all three had taken care of children. They were kind and understanding. One is a man. We trained them all. The man is on duty on the weekend. He takes us shopping. The people really have to be dedicated. The pay is two dollars and seventy-five cents an hour to care for one person, three dollars and twenty-five cents for two people. No medical coverage, no paid vacations, no paid sick days. Also no withholding, though, and I imagine some of these people cheat on their taxes. But they're getting the same salaries as someone who takes care of an old person. Our needs are somewhat greater."

While the supply of people to do the work is abundant, reliable attendants are scarce. Stories have circulated through the handicapped community of attendants who have sedated quadriplegics and gone out for the day, who have been insubordinate, who have pilfered food money. The disabled people have often done nothing in retaliation, out of fear that their attendants, bad as they are, will leave and they will be left alone.

"It's a big problem," Ira said. "Understand, it's not a maid service we're talking about. It's not someone coming in to clean the carpet. In this case, we're the carpet. It's our bodies they're taking care of."

We had some lunch. I was served a bacon, lettuce, and tomato sandwich on toast, along with some coleslaw and another beer. The same was brought the Hollands. The man who takes the Hollands shopping had come by to feed Vicki, while the attendant on duty, a cordial woman named Jessie, fed Ira. It was the first time I had ever sat down to enjoy a meal with people this handicapped. Other quadriplegics had at least been able to feed themselves. It was a little unsettling to watch people so many years my senior being fed like babies, their mouths wiped with a napkin when some food dribbled down. A mixture of pity for them and gratefulness for my own health was my initial reaction, and then the sentiment was gone. Although they had their limitations, they were coping. They were happy. The meal was pleasant.

After lunch, I suggested the Hollands take me on a tour around the island, as physical proof of its accessibility to people who couldn't open a door on their own. They readily agreed. We left the cool, air-conditioned apartment and ventured outside. Jessie remained in the apartment to clean up. She wouldn't be needed, the Hollands tried to assure me. I wasn't at all comforted by this, wondering how I would handle any mishap, though I decided it was best not to worry excessively about it.

In hot, muggy muck, we moved down Main Street, bordered by U-shaped buildings and gorgeous trees. The Hollands set a brisk pace. Since Vicki has some limited movement in her hands, she uses a hand-controlled electric wheelchair. Ira has no such ability; he rides in a chair that responds to sipping and puffing on a pneumatic tube. On the sides of both Ira's and Vicki's chairs were decals with the word "Love."

Although the island has just one street, it has two walkways, one on each side of Main Street, that stretch along the water. We headed down to the pathway nearest the Hollands' apartment house. It was deserted, except for some birds and an attractive young woman sunbathing on a blanket. She was comely in a black, low-scooped bathing suit. A red scarf bandannaed her brown hair. She paid us no mind as we clattered along, admiring the shimmering pink water under a sun that glazed the trees.

"That big ugly hunk over there is Big Alice, the Con Ed plant," Ira said. "Just what everyone ought to have in his backyard. You've got to admit it's an eyesore, but at least we still have the water to look at."

"It's pretty here in the summer," Vicki said. "Ira and I sit out here quite a bit. We read, talk, sometimes fall sound asleep."

"Yes," Ira put in, "you don't have to worry much about somebody shoving you into the drink."

Yawning, the woman in the black bikini got up, brushed herself off, slipped into some beach thongs, rolled up her blanket, and scuffled back to her apartment. She smiled in a placatory way as she bustled past.

Vicki said, "People here have become aware that disabled people are out in the world and they either accept them or reject them. I think if they accept them, they do better than if they make believe they don't exist."

Ira said, "Some people here have told me that they had never been exposed to disabled individuals before. They told me, 'You know, from across the street, they look very weird. But when you talk to them, they're just like anybody else. It's been a learning experience.'"

"A great majority of the people here are absolutely fantastic," Vicki said. "Some don't like us. We don't like everybody, either."

We breezed back to Main Street. We came upon Bigelow's Pharmacy. Its original store, in Manhattan, is New York's oldest pharmacy. This was one of New York's newest pharmacies.

"Let's go in," Vicki said to me.

Ira decided to wait outside. "I don't go in much for drug-store junk — hair creams, curlers, permanents," he said. "Yuk!"

Bigelow's had electronic doors, so as soon as Vicki's wheel-chair crossed the mat fronting the place, the doors hummed open. Electronic doors seem made for the severely disabled. Inside, the aisles were extra wide, making it fairly simple for Vicki to roll through them.

"You see, it's as easy for me to pick out my goods as it is for you," she said as she spun down one of the aisles. "You ought to see the difference in Manhattan stores, not to men-tion in stores in much of the country. Take a shopping cart into your local drugstore some time and see how easy it is to get around. You'll be knocking down everything in sight."

An elderly woman in blue jeans and a T-shirt was thumb-ing through the cartons of hair colorings.

"Hi, Vicki, how are you?" she said.

"Just fine," Vicki replied. "How are you?"

"I'll be okay as soon as I find a decent hair coloring," the woman said.

"Keep it natural," Vicki said.

We left the pharmacy, rejoined Ira, and whirled across the way to the Chapel of the Good Shepherd. It dates back to 1889 but was restored in 1975. Among other things, ramps were added, as well as an elevator to carry wheelchairs to the second floor, where services and meetings are held.

"It's all denominations," Ira said. "Catholic, Protestant, Jewish, atheist."

A young man and young woman in wheelchairs were yammering just outside the chapel. Snatches of the conversa-tion I overheard could have come from any teenage couple working up the possibility of a first date.

"So how do you feel about a movie Sunday?" the young man asked sheepishly, presumably able to summon the courage to ask only because he had chosen Sunday rather than Saturday night. Certainly he could not reasonably expect the young lady — any young lady — to be free on Saturday night.

"That sounds nice," the woman said.

"Does *Bound for Glory* interest you?"

"Sure, why not."

"All right, I'll talk to you."

With that, the young man quickly scooted off, as if hurrying to spread the hot news to the boys back in the dorm.

The Hollands and I swung away from the chapel and ambled farther down Main Street. For a moment, the air seemed more sweltering than it had all day; then a sudden cool breeze swept over us and made our heads light.

"Hello, hello," a beefy man in a Lacoste sportshirt said to Ira and Vicki.

"Hi, Phil," Ira said.

Vicki just gave him a small smile.

"You guys are looking good," the man said.

"No complaints," Ira said. "I've been doing quite a bit of jogging."

We drifted past a row of stores. Cards 'n Gifts, advertising ice cream, shakes, floats. The dry cleaner. The Roosevelt Island Delicatessen. Manufacturers Hanover Trust. ("That's where we keep the loot," Ira said.)

We got to the Grog Shop. "This is the local, indispensable liquor store," Ira said. "Without this, everyone would go berserk. We've got no bars here, but we've got a liquor store. Our apartments become our bars. Within reason, of course."

We paused outside the Grog Shop, which appeared to be doing the healthiest business of any store we had passed. A bony man, legs like stilts, shirt hanging out over his trousers, stumbled out of the liquor store, a foaming beer bottle in his hand. Ira screwed up his face like he'd swallowed something sour. "This is not what I mean by within reason," he said.

Ira began to speak about transportation. Since New York's subways and buses and taxis aren't accessible to the handicapped, the mobility problem thus far has been answered by a bustling and profitable van industry. As it happens, the Hollands are lucky enough to own their own van, the gift of a friend, though often no one is available to drive it. When that happens, they are forced to rely on commercial operations. Dozens of van services have sprung up in the New York metropolitan area, as well as in other big cities, to shuttle around the disabled. They range from one-man-and-a-van affairs to fleets of fifty-odd vehicles. In many areas, the industry is unregulated. That poses problems. In New York City, for instance, Ira pointed out, fares are fixed at twenty-eight dollars round-trip to any hospital in the city. Medicaid picks up the tab. However, fares for any other trips — to work, to a friend's, to the movies — are set by the van companies. And the cost is borne by the disabled person. Fares are frequently three or four times taxi rates. Ira and Vicki said they have spent anywhere from forty to seventy-five dollars just to get across the bridge into Manhattan. Three years ago, they ventured to Cold Spring, New York — about a sixty-mile drive — to drop in on a friend. The driver socked them for ninety-five dollars.

"Since he couldn't go back to the city and then return and retrieve us, I couldn't very well tell him to go sit in the corner and eat some tree," Ira said. "So I asked him if he wanted something to eat. He ate everything but the table. I asked him if he wanted a drink of scotch. I didn't know he would drink the bottle."

Vans aren't necessarily merely a nuisance; they are sometimes a threat to health. Safety standards often aren't well enforced. Therefore, the ceilings frequently are too low for someone propped up in a wheelchair. Locking devices to fasten the chairs in place are sometimes nonexistent. Wheelchairs flip over. Heads get bumped. Bones get broken. One time, Ira was being backed down from a van that had too low a ceiling. His head caught above the door. Oblivious to the problem, the driver kept tugging at the chair. "If a security guard hadn't spotted what was happening, my neck would have been broken and I would now be a statistic," Ira said. "These guys are making a fortune and they're taking our lives in their hands. It's an outrage. When most people go out to dinner, they consider the price of the restaurant. To us, the restaurant is nothing. By the time we get there, we've spent forty-five dollars and we may not be alive to eat."

(I subsequently got in touch with Medicab Incorporated of New York, based in Yonkers. It's one of the biggest van services, with forty vans, and it has franchises in Kansas City, New Orleans, Philadelphia, Bloomfield, New Jersey, and Queens. Morton Schiowitz, the chief executive officer, insists that industry rates are quite reasonable. Van services incur high costs, he said, especially because getting someone in a wheelchair into and out of a van consumes a lot of time. Time is money. "I'm sure that in some instances extremely high rates have been charged," he said. "But generally I don't think that our rates are exorbitant. Unfortunately, the fare is being levied to the person least able to afford it. Often, I feel very guilty charging some of these people these rates. But there should be some sort of subsidy for them. We can't operate any cheaper." Medicab equips its vans with locking devices, though Schiowitz acknowledged that some operations don't. "Better policing of safety is essential," he said. "Otherwise, the handicapped person is at the mercy of the driver and the van.")

The Hollands and I drifted to the far edge of the island, across from Sloan's supermarket, to check out their garden. They belong to the garden club.

"It's the second one in," Ira said. "It starts with the zucchini and ends with the corn."

Vicki invited me to take a zucchini home. "Take a big one," she implored. "Make sure it's a big one."

Next, we headed back toward the Hollands' apartment house. We passed a beefy, ruddy-faced man. "Here come the hot-rodders," he laughed. "How come Ira's always got the lead?"

"Only when you see us," Vicki said. "He's usually chasing after me."

As we went farther down the street, a man on a motor-bike sputtered by. "Hey, you get those dang chairs off the street," he called out jokingly.

"After you dump that bike," Ira said.

We paused in the courtyard of the Hollands' building, then bounded down to Blackwell Park. "Let's sit here a bit," Ira said. We sat there, enveloped by a soft late afternoon breeze. We savored the breeze, the combed lawn, the "walk" we had just had. Two tugboats plowed down the East River.

"I hope you noticed," Ira said, "that all during this tour you didn't need to help us once. We left our attendant in the apartment, remember? If you hadn't been here, we would have been able to do everything the same, except for picking that zucchini. That's what we mean about this place. It's not like this across the bridge. It's not like this in most of the country. Look at us out here, sitting and watching the boats and the children. Feeling the sun. In a little bit, we'll say good-bye to you, then go on in. Dinner will be ready soon. Maybe we'll make some phone calls. Get some sleep. Do we really ask for so much?"

Another day with the Hollands. Winter, this time. I wanted to know more about the social life of the Hollands, how people so severely disabled found entertainment. They had told me that on weekends they invariably trooped into Manhattan to catch a movie and, afterwards, to grab a bite to eat. I had asked if I could go along with them sometime, and they gladly said yes.

The day was dank and cool, though not as cold as it had been. Old snow, stained at the bases of trees and pockmarked by rain, was on the ground, though the walks were clear. The plan was to take in *Blue Country,* a new French film playing in Manhattan, then to have dinner at a Chinese restaurant in Queens. I got to the Hollands' apartment at around 11:30, and they were already dressed to go. The attendant on duty was a busty woman named Martha. Her hair, long and black, was tied back with a ribbon at the nape of her neck. A friend, Ed Lichter, a tall, spare man with scraggly whiskers, was going to take the Hollands in their van. Ira was bundled up in a green ski vest, big brown mittens, a green ski mask, and a long navy blue cape. Vicki had on a short fake-fur coat with a hood.

Ira introduced Martha and Ed. Ed, who's in his mid-twenties, works in Goldwater Hospital as a "medical utilization review analyst," a long-winded way of saying somebody who reviews patients' benefit charts. He had been a clerk at an insurance firm when he met Ira. Ira cottoned to him and aided him in finding a job at Goldwater. In gratitude, Ed does a lot of favors for the Hollands, including taking them into the city whenever they want to go and he's not working. "What I do for Ira and Vicki is strictly friendship," he told me. "No money is involved." He hesitated, then added, "I have a dream. My dream is that someday people like Ira and Vicki will no longer be thought of as strange."

We moseyed out to the van. It was a standard Dodge Sportsman, with some special modifications. The back seat had been shoved all the way to the rear to make room for two wheelchairs. A small winch was used to yank Ira and Vicki up a ramp and into the van. They don't look it, but motorized chairs with respirators and people in them weigh upward of six hundred pounds. Clamps had been installed to hold the chairs in place, and special seat belts looped around the chairs. The Hollands affectionately refer to the van as "Elizabeth," after a young Swedish woman they had fleetingly met in Goldwater. "She was one of those people who come into your life and then you never see them again," Vicki said. "But she was an exceptionally wonderful person. She treated us as if we were gold."

Ed loaded Ira and Vicki onto the van, using the winch, which made an enormous racket. He got in and we drove off into Queens and then over the Queensboro Bridge into Manhattan. We tooled past an immense Silvercup factory ("The World's Finest Bread," a billboard proclaimed). As we rumbled into Manhattan, traffic got heavy. Long, snaking lines of cars, one behind the other, leap-frog fashion, spangled the roads. Honking horns. The roads were bad. Deep potholes. Ira and Vicki were doing okay, though, strapped in as they were. "In one of those van services," Vicki said, "by now we would probably be dead."

"Now, if you'll notice," Ira said, "nine out of ten blocks have no curb cuts. That means that somebody in a wheelchair can't possibly cross the street unless someone happens to be around to help. And with chairs this heavy, that someone better be Superman. The rule is that if the city puts in a new sidewalk, curb cuts are added. More often than not, however, they'll put in driveways rather than curb cuts. The difference is that a driveway has edges to it. It might as well be a curb. A cut must be totally level and smooth, or else we'll tip over."

Ed got bogged down behind a barrier that had been erected smack in the middle of First Avenue and had to back up. A woman driver was directly behind us. Beep.

"Who is she to get all hopped up?" Ira said. "Let her take a powder."

Beep. Beep.

With difficulty, Ed finally managed to extract himself from the muddle, though the woman couldn't resist firing one more honk.

"I just wish I could hop out and bust her in the chops," Ira shouted. His eyeballs bulged like muscles. "I hate these people who only want to push others around. They want to push you down until you're practically owned by them. Hate 'em. Hate 'em. Hate 'em."

Cooled down, Ira swiveled his head toward Vicki. "Did you tell Martha when we'd be back?"

"Yeah, I said late," Vicki said.

"She'll probably eat us out of the house. She can handle about eighty pounds of cold cuts."

"Martha eats a lot?" I asked.

"Let's put it this way," Ira said. "She'll never die of starvation. We'd need to use the winch to get her into this van."

Ed parked across the street from the theater, in front of Oscar's Salt of the Sea Restaurant. Ramp down. Hooks unfastened. Seat belts off. Ed wheeled Vicki down the ramp. No curb cuts were in sight, so Ed pulled Vicki's chair back on two wheels and heaved her onto the sidewalk. He rested a moment, then repeated the procedure with Ira.

Just as Ira's chair landed on the sidewalk, the power on it inexplicably failed and the respirator died. Concerned, Ed crouched down to inspect the wires. Fortunately, Ira knew a way of breathing artificially, called "frog breathing." His respiratory system doesn't work. About thirty or forty years ago, a polio patient who shall remain nameless, mostly because no one knows who he or she is, discovered accidentally but fortuitously that you can breathe artificially. You close off your nose, then force air down into your lungs by rapid movement of your tongue. It's called glossopharyngeal breathing. It's awfully difficult to learn. If you're proficient at it, you can pick it up in several months. Some people are never able to master it. It's tiring, no matter how adept you are at it, and it's hard for someone to keep at for very long.

"What if you didn't know how to frog breathe?" I asked Ira out on the sidewalk.

"I would die," he said bluntly. "Frankly, I would die."

Ed fiddled with different wires, tried a spare respirator that had been carted along. No luck. He flagged down a passing tow truck to see if the driver could help. The tow truck driver took one look at the two wheelchairs, shook his head and drove on. Ira was tense to the edges of rage.

"The bastard," Ed sneered.

"I think we'd better go back," Ira said. Restless, impatient, he cursed his luck. "Christ, this is ridiculous. What a goddamned bummer."

Ira and Vicki were rolled back into the van. "I think we're destined not to see this movie," Ira said. "This is the third time we set out to see it. The first time, the van broke down. The second time, Vicki and I had a fight."

"It's probably not as good as they say," Vicki put in.

"Actually," Ed said, "Ira planned this to make sure Martha wouldn't eat everything."

We retraced our route back to Roosevelt Island. Conversation was scarce and tended to be snappish. Dolly Parton thundered from the radio. Ed tapped his fingers against the steering wheel.

We got back to the apartment and had some hot chocolate. Martha stirred the steamy brew and stuck straws in the mugs so that Ira and Vicki could sip without help.

"I'm really annoyed," Ira said. "I'd like to get up and kick the damn chair." His face was flushed with anger.

"Now, Ira," Vicki said soothingly. "There you go again."

Ed hoisted out of the closet a cardboard carton with wires and various electrical gadgets. Sprawled out on the carpet, he went to work on the chair. In a few minutes he discovered the problem: a wire had jiggled loose. He fastened it.

"Son of a bitch," Ira said. "We ought to carry this stuff with us."

Ed said, "We will from now on."

While we finished our hot chocolate, Ira and Vicki chatted about the problems of getting into movie theaters. Many theaters, they pointed out, have steps or escalators. No good. Most newer theaters, it was their experience, were inaccessible. Older theaters tended to be better.

Vicki said, "We haven't been able to see some films we've wanted to see, because they never come to an accessible theater. Like *Julia*. Oh, did we want to see that. We called up a theater where it was playing and were told to come on over, they had an elevator. Well, we got there — and to get into the lobby you have to go up four steps. Two steps are too much. And these were big steps. They were like a ladder. Ed went in and asked the manager what the story was. We'd been told we didn't have to negotiate any steps. 'You don't,' he told Ed, 'once you get into the lobby.' The thing is, people don't think. If you're not handicapped, steps aren't a hazard and so you don't notice them."

Around three, we decided to go out to dinner after all.

Ira and Vicki were bundled up again, I slipped on my coat, and we straggled down to the van.

"Martha, don't expect us," Ira said as he clacked out the door. "Because if something else happens, I'm staying there. I speak Chinese."

Tooling along in the van, Ed said, "We just had this repaired, so it runs wonderfully."

"Which is more than we can say for some people," Vicki said.

"Rub it in," Ira said. "Go on and rub it in."

"We've got twelve miles today on this already," Ed said, eyeing the odometer.

"All that for a cup of hot chocolate," Ira said. "Yuk! The gasoline industry must love people like us."

We hurtled through Jackson Heights, Queens. Past where the houses began to thin out, we swerved into a parking lot, where the China Chef restaurant was nestled amid a jumble of stores. As we pulled in, a couple of kids pelted the side of the van with snowballs.

"Oh, I'd like to beat them up," Ira snarled.

"Calm down," Vicki said. "They do that to everyone."

Ed rolled Vicki and Ira down the ramp. We stamped along the pavement of the parking lot toward the restaurant, watching ahead to avoid the patches of ice, keeping our heads down against the shoving cold. The wheelchairs clattered along as they struck bumps in the pavement. Wheelchairs aren't equipped with suspensions. Now and then Ira or Vicki hit a particularly nasty mound and Ed had to push them upright in the seat.

No curb cuts had been put into the sidewalk fronting the restaurant, so Ed shoved the chairs over the curb. He let out a long breath when he was done. He looked pooped.

"Don't worry, Ed," Ira said. "We're intending to enter you

in the weight-lifting competition in the next Olympics. You should walk away with the prize."

It was an unposh restaurant, with tacky velvet wallpaper and elaborate chandeliers. The manager had been called ahead of time and expected us. He greeted us at the door and motioned us to the back of the restaurant, where there was enough room to squeeze in two wheelchairs. Scattered through the restaurant were about a dozen people, forking down Moo Goo Gai Pan, Beef with Bean Sprouts, Chicken with Chinese Vegetables. As we moved past, I watched the faces of the people in the booths. Some of them paid us no mind. We did not seem to matter. I did see several jaws drop, as if to say, "Well, what will they let in here next. We're going to have to find a new place."

Ed removed Vicki's coat. Her wheelchair motor was still running.

"Hey, Vicki, turn off your chair," Ira said, "or you'll end up in the kitchen."

"I think I'd prefer the bar."

A crew of waiters huddled together nearby, watching the table and muttering something in Chinese.

"I imagine they're saying, 'So how do we decide who gets them?'" Ira whispered. "Do we draw eggrolls, or do we have a Mu Shi Pork fight?' "

The manager finally came over to take our order. He was extremely cordial.

"Let me ask you," Ira said, "do you get many people here in wheelchairs?"

"No," the manager said. "But you call ahead and I make room and I try to have you have a good time. I welcome anybody."

We ordered four dishes and agreed to share them. Ed was to feed Vicki. I was sitting next to Ira.

"You'll feed me," Ira said to me. I had never fed anybody, not even a baby, and felt somewhat unnerved about feeding a man. But why not?

"Since you're feeding me," Ira said, "do you mind washing your hands? I'm not trying to be rude. It's just my Jewish up-bringing showing."

I retreated to the men's room, washed, and returned in time to find our order. I dished out some food onto Ira's plate, then filled my own. I alternated giving him a forkful and downing some myself. It worked out smoothly. I got over my unease.

The conversation ranged far and wide. Ira is always wound up and ready to let go with a small speech on any subject — Vietnam, the oppression of blacks, religious hy-pocrisy — any subject, minor or massive.

We talked of books we had read, films we had seen. The movie *One Flew Over the Cuckoo's Nest* entered the con-versation. Everyone agreed it was a first-rate film, a searing commentary that cut deep into the emotions. I mentioned how brutal the conditions were in the asylum pictured in the movie.

"We know how bad it can be," Vicki said. "It's that bad. That bad, or worse."

Ira said, "We wanted everyone to choke that nurse. Choke her till she was squirming and begging for mercy. See, we had a bitch just like her at Goldwater. She gave us this big speech one day. She told us there were no more Florence Nightingales, so don't look for them. If your sheets get changed, consider yourself fortunate. If they don't, consider yourself lucky that you're here. You could be dead."

The hours whirled by. We were all stuffed. Much food re-mained on plates.

"I told you we should have brought Martha," Ira said. "She

would have eaten everything, including the sugar. She might have left the pepper."

The check came. "You know, Ed gets a commission to take us here," Vicki said. "Every time we ask to go out, Ed takes us here. Rain, snow, sleet, we come here."

"We've been here eight thousand, seven hundred and ninety-two times," Ira said.

Ed gave Vicki her medication — four pills and a liquid antacid. He passed the same dosage to me to give to Ira.

After successfully getting the medication down, Ira told me, "You're very good at this. If Martha leaves, I'll give you a call."

Ed dressed Vicki and Ira. It was tricky slipping Ira's ski vest on.

"It was really funny when we bought this vest," Ed said. "At first, we went to a J. C. Penney and tried to get a conventional ski jacket."

"Yeah," Ira interrupted, "and this salesman tried putting it on me like my arm was made of rubber. So I started yelling, 'Hey, what the hell are you doing? That's an arm there, buddy, not a sausage.' The man dropped the vest and broke out into this profuse sweat. Then he said, 'I'm leaving here to sell boats.'"

"Well, he sort of said that," Ed put in. "We went over to Herman's and told the salesman there that Ira had tried to ski down Mount Everest and didn't make it. The man was very, very nice to him."

Ira began to tell some slightly off-color stories. Vicki laughed and reproached him. A doggie bag with leftovers was deposited on the table, and we took our leave.

The lot was lined with cars. Melted snow ran in the gutters. The huge tires of buses roared past. It was the last hour of light. We piled, or were piled, into the van and took off. We were silent for a while; the only noise was the whining of the motor. Ed rubbed his cheek against the grain of his whiskers, making a gentle crackling sound. Ira screwed up his face, making calculations of some sort, trying to conjure up, apparently, some sort of summary statement. Turning toward me, he said, "I can't help but think of all the people in the world being bullied, pushed around. I'm appalled that a lot of people are up in arms about how much we want. You read about how so-called intelligent people are so surprised or outraged by our protest. These well-to-do people, living out there in their comfortable suburban homes, what do they know about our needs. Oh, everyone will act polite in front of us and make these nice statements about how important it is to provide the proper accommodations for us. But deep down they're thinking, what's come over you people that you think you have the right to argue with us on these matters. Our business is to make the decisions, your business is to accept whatever the hell we decide. Well, we're not going to keep our tiny little mouths shut and follow orders."

Ira and Vicki invited me back to the apartment for coffee, but I begged off. It was getting late. They said they wanted to have me over for dinner in a few weeks, maybe see that movie already, and I agreed to come. I was dropped off near a subway station, and as I said good-bye, Ira threw in a final thought.

"I suppose we seem to be asking a lot of society," he said. "In some ways, perhaps we are. But not that much. Not that much at all. We just want to get by. We don't want mansions, we don't want yachts, nor do we want pity. We just want a life like everyone else. We live a civilized existence. I guess we do. If we didn't, they would probably shoot people like us."

9

I ASKED Leslie Milk whether employers were warming to the idea of hiring the handicapped. Milk replied, "Well, I suppose they are warming, but at the rate that a pot of water warms when you hold a match under it. We're making some progress. But it's disgustingly slow." Yet Milk didn't seem totally depressed about it. "Fighting job discrimination by nature is very frustrating work. At this point, we're inured to frustration. We are not going to shut up."

Milk is executive director of Mainstream Incorporated, which is a Washington outfit that sprang up to get companies to hire the handicapped. The organization is the product of the mind of one man. His name is Harold Krents. Krents was born blind. The suburban elementary school near his parents' home at first refused to accept him, classifying him an "ungraded student," which meant he could have some desk space but could not be included in the student enrollment listing. Krents felt himself lucky, since many disabled students he knew of never managed to get past the door of a public school. In time, he graduated cum laude in English from Harvard College, then picked up a law degree at Harvard Law School. He spent a year at Oxford. Credentials enough for a beginning, he thought, but all employers saw was Krents' blindness. Forty law firms turned him down. One company issued a letter of rejection on the mere rumor that he was contemplating applying. At last, the firm of Surrey, Karasik and Morse took a chance on him. "And the only accommodation needed was a full-time secretary. Otherwise I pull my oar like every other lawyer in the company." Disconcerted by the humbling experience of finding a job, Krents decided to put together an organization that might smooth the way for other handicapped people. In 1975, Mainstream came into being, employing a dozen people. Harold Krents's life story went on to inspire the successful play and movie *Butterflies Are Free.*

The most prevalent troubles of handicapped people who have carved out a self-reliant life have to do with getting a job to pay the cost of their freedom. The best available evidence indicates that between forty and fifty percent of the handicapped deemed qualified to work are unemployed, more than in any minority. A sizable number of those who hold jobs are underemployed. Typically, they work in shelter workshops, grinding out wicker furniture or light bulbs for meager wages. The consulting firm of Arthur D. Little conducted a study for the Department of Health, Education and Welfare and found that of all people with "mobility limiting conditions" who had been judged employable, less than half were in fact working. Steven Jamison, a consultant for IBM, undertook a study that, in contrasting the disabled with the total population of employable people, found the handicapped undereducated (forty percent finished high school versus fifty-six percent of the general population; five percent finished college versus nine percent), underemployed (fifty-eight percent of men were employed, versus seventy-six percent) and underpaid (thirty-one percent of men earned $7,000 or more, versus forty-six percent).

From executive suites in New York, Atlanta, Los Angeles,

Chicago — the business communities of the country — the handicapped are watched with unease, not to mention with contempt and fear. They are widely looked upon with low esteem, and rarely the reverse, since almost no employer in the country is shy to put the slam (at least in private) on anybody he thinks can't do the job.

"I applaud their determination, but let's face it, they're limited."

"We're not a charitable organization. We're a business. I can't take any risks."

"It takes a peculiar type of individual to overcome a serious handicap and hold a job. It's not easy finding that person, and how am I to judge?"

"The government hasn't even made it clear just who constitutes a handicapped person. Is somebody with blood pressure of 150 handicapped? Beats me. I could make a hero out of myself by hiring people with blood pressure of 150 and then crowing that, hey, I'm hiring the handicapped by the truckload."

"There's no reason for this stupidity," Leslie Milk told me. She is an engaging, extremely talkative woman with a high-pitched voice. "All the evidence we have of employment performance of the disabled suggests that employers should be out there bidding for them like football teams chasing after first draft picks." She mentioned a study done by the Du Pont Company that sought to measure job performance, safety records, and attendance of the company's disabled force. Du Pont employs more than a hundred thousand workers in the United States, roughly fifteen hundred of them physically handicapped. Their job titles range up and down the corporate ladder, from laborers to managers. So far as safety is concerned, fifty-one percent of the disabled workers proved to be above average; just four percent were below average. In attendance, seventy-nine percent were average or above. In job performance, rated by their supervisors, thirty-seven percent came out above average and just nine percent were below average. What's more, the study showed that the nature of the handicap didn't prevent workers from doing good jobs. Some of the best performers had the most severe handicaps.

"One of the common misconceptions," Milk said, "is that it will cost the moon to accommodate a handicapped worker. The fact is, making buildings accessible is cheaper than anyone imagines. The Kaiser Aluminum and Chemical Corporation had architects go through its headquarters building and they concluded that making it barrier-free would cost one hundred and sixty thousand dollars. We sent in architects and calculated that the building could be made reasonably accessible for just eight thousand dollars. The company was going to make every floor totally accessible — every bathroom, every door, every hallway. That's hardly necessary unless everyone in the company is disabled."

Mainstream figured out that commercial and industrial buildings can be made accessible for no more than a penny a square foot, less than companies spend to clean and polish vinyl floors. It came to this conclusion after studying thirty corporate facilities, ranging from huge petrochemical plants to small sales offices and stores. The costs went from $920 to make a 26,000-square-foot food processing plant accessible, to $21,500 for a six-million-square-foot metal refinery.

Milk made these additional points about the hiring of the handicapped:

"Most companies are still far behind where they ought to be. That's because we've never had a strong federal presence, and I'm not sure how strong that presence is now. Companies

don't understand who the handicapped are. We need more
places like ours to tell them.

"Generally speaking, I don't think the business community
is interested in hiring the handicapped. Many managers
fear the disabled worker can't do the job. The prejudice is
out of the realm of words. Let's face it, the image of the
handicapped in this country is that of a poster child.

"I can understand something about what employers are
facing when they think of hiring a disabled candidate. It's
a scary proposition. You'll be sitting across from a quadriplegic, and you'll be thinking not about whether he could
do the job, but about what you can do to avoid what happened to him. And the longer you look at him, the scarier
it gets."

What good has Mainstream done? For the most part, the
company doesn't "try to shove handicapped workers down
the unwilling throats of employers," as Leslie Milk puts it.
It styles itself as a consultant, to which a booming number of
companies have been flocking. Place a call to its toll-free hot
line, or make a personal visit, and an outpouring of advice
on whatever you need to know about complying with the law
will be supplied. Lists of agencies through which handicapped workers can be sought are available. An architectural
firm is on call to make building inspections at cost. Also,
under a contract from the Department of Labor, Mainstream
is staging seminars across the country to explain the law.

A favorite aphorism of Mainstream's is that businesses
operate on the theory of spending as little money as possible
and so the only hope for the handicapped is strong enforcement of the law. Milk said to me when I called on her, "I
think we've demonstrated to a lot of people that it's not hard
or expensive to hire the handicapped. But the route is long

and tortuous. We're not sure how much of our advice is being followed. We are trying to build a bridge that the handicapped can cross to get to the world of employment, and a lot of cables have to be strung. Our ultimate success is tied to how much the government enforces the law." At first, Milk said, she was dismayed that the Department of Labor, the body charged with enforcing employment aspects of the Rehabilitation Act, was only reacting to discrimination complaints lodged with it. You can't wait for complaints, is her belief. Companies ignore laws. You have to hold a gun to them. Beginning in the summer of 1978, the department branched wide from its original preoccupation and began to initiate spot checks. It has set a probably overly ambitious goal of annually looking at the practices of twenty percent of the twenty-nine thousand prime contractors pocketing dollars from the labor department. The need for this was baldly demonstrated by the early returns. Of the first three hundred companies that were reviewed, the preponderance were not in sight of full compliance.

"One of the toughest problems coming up now is the plight of the individual with invisible handicaps," Milk told me. "The paraplegic with a degree in astrophysics, I suspect, is going to get hired. The assembly-line worker with a history of epileptic fits is not. One of the reasons is that there aren't as many psychic benefits for the employer hiring someone who doesn't look handicapped. If they have to hire handicapped workers, many employers seem to feel, then they want to feel good about it."

In mid-1974, GTE Sylvania, the electronics and light bulb people, refused to hire fifty-three-year-old Lawrence Katz for a technical writing job. Company doctors said that his treatment a year earlier for Hodgkin's disease made him a poor insurance risk. Disgruntled and unable to land another position, Katz filed a complaint with the Department of Labor, charging discrimination against the disabled. Six months later, after lengthy discussions with Labor Department specialists, the company hired Katz. The case was one of the first conciliated under the Rehabilitation Act. Small and spread out they may be, but a number of companies have begun to make hiring concessions. Sylvania has also done away with weight limits it used to have for all jobs. ITT has disposed of rules that prohibited applicants with epilepsy, cancer, and some other health problems. An epileptic has been hired as a packer for an ITT subsidiary. Officials of Continental Illinois National Bank and Trust Company in Chicago came up with a braille version of its computer-programming aptitude test, because they feared that a blind applicant was about to complain under the federal law. He got the job. The Union Carbide Corporation is advertising sales representative job openings in handicapped groups' newspapers, specifying only that "car maneuverability" is required. U.S. Steel has done recruiting at the National Technical Institute for the Deaf. General Motors claims to employ 25,000 disabled workers out of its total force of 580,000. Since 1942, IBM has had formal programs to train and hire the handicapped. Teletypewriters are put into the office and home of any of its deaf employees. Optical scanners are bought for blind employees. Parking places are reserved for handicapped workers. Interpreters are hired for deaf employees attending meetings. One woman has a desk outfitted with bell boxes and a special contraption called a "braille cell" that helps her find her place at the typewriter after she's interrupted herself to pick up the phone.

More than 3.5 million disabled veterans live in the United States, nearly half of them combatants in World War II, and almost 490,000 of them veterans of Vietnam. A great many are severely handicapped, and thousands came home totally disabled. Information on what has happened to the wounded soldiers is sketchy, but nobody quarrels with the assumption that most of them are probably unemployed. They are all clients of the Veterans Administration, one of the largest bureaucracies in the government. It operates 171 hospitals and numberless programs in areas such as education, pension, insurance, home loans, and burial. Taxpayers support it to the tune of $20 billion a year. The VA's current administrator, Max Cleland, is handicapped himself. Both of his legs and an arm were blown off in a Vietnam explosion. Since his appointment, Cleland has spoken passionately on behalf of disabled veterans: "It's bad enough to shut these handicapped men and women out of the economic system of the country they served. It's intolerable to waste their tremendous remaining potential on the basis of disabilities they incurred in that service."

But Cleland has yet to do much for the flood of severely wounded soldiers. The VA boasts that it is one of the biggest employers of the handicapped. Thirty-eight thousand of its 225,000 employees are disabled; fourteen thousand are disabled veterans. War-made paraplegics are well provided for in terms of cash; a soldier with one hundred percent physical disability gets the equivalent of $25,000 a year. Yet many of the severely wounded lack education and work experience. The VA has done little to set them on paths toward useful careers. Estimates suggest that as many as eighty percent of the paralyzed are unemployed today. Some of them have committed suicide.

Some good, it appears, has originated from a pressure group, the Disabled American Veterans, that watches VA policy-making and performance with hound-dog tenacity. Formed in 1920, with headquarters in Cincinnati and Washington, the DAV boasts 550,000 members, every one a veteran with a service-related disability. Much of its recent strength has come from Vietnam veterans, who now comprise twenty-three percent of total membership. In a typical year, the DAV manages to introduce fifty-odd bills into Congress through legislators friendly to its cause. Of the smattering that passed recently, one raised the amount of compensation for veterans, another extended grants for special housing to more disabled veterans and increased pay to widows of veterans who die of service-related disabilities.

But it, too, recognizes that most of the country's disabled veterans still languish unhappily, with nothing much to live for. It has filed roughly a hundred complaints against corporations, universities, hospitals, and the like. "We will fight discrimination against these vets on all levels — federal, state and local — if we feel the causes are sound," a DAV official said to me. "The unemployment rate of disabled veterans is a sin. We won't sit still till we wipe out that sin."

Most handicapped people I talked to said that they have always dreamed a great deal about holding good jobs, but many said those dreams were fading now. I spoke with a young, attractive woman in California who had a progressive eye disease that was cutting off her vision at the same time that deafness was closing in on her. She was no longer able to drive, and you had to speak almost at a shout for her to hear you. I found myself often having to repeat myself two or three times. But she didn't look disabled. She complained that she was having no luck finding work. In desperation, she said, she was trying to get one of the traditional jobs that handicapped people are able to find, such as counseling other disabled people. "Now, I'm being discriminated against for not being disabled enough," she said. "Employers glance at me and I just don't look handicapped. They want people in wheelchairs and all that. You know what my husband said last night? He said, 'Why don't you maim yourself a little?'" An aspiring filmmaker who dove off a dock into three feet of water and broke his neck said he had made the rounds of movie companies and had gotten nothing but cordial rejections. "A lot of my friends went to these same places and got work," he told me. "And I had a pretty good sample reel. In entertainment, it's very easy to say, 'Well, you're not right for us.' It's very subjective anyway. But I know my work is as good as my friends'. I should be working." He chewed on his fingernails and stared out the window at the dark sky. "All that stuff builds up inside you," he said, "and then it turns into hatred."

In a flinty office building sandwiched between skyscrapers in the run-down commercial district of Manhattan, I met a woman named Sandra Schnur. She is a small, soft-spoken, middle-aged woman, with a touching, uncalculating friendliness. She has a shrewd and watchful look. Since the age of fifteen, she has been paralyzed from the neck down. She has limited movement in her hands. She can use a Touch-Tone phone (though she can't hold the phone to her ear), type on an electric typewriter, and operate an electric wheelchair. She is not able to shake hands.

Schnur worked for the city coordinating New York's public transit half-fare program for the handicapped. In the outer room of the office, I found routine cacophony: a large open space as aswarm with bodies as the floor of a stock exchange, paper in motion everywhere, women hugging telephones, sporadic bursts of typing. Schnur nodded for me to follow her to a quiet cubicle where we could talk. We went to a small chipped brown desk; some chairs were set near the windows.

Schnur learned that she had polio in 1950. Doctors told her that if she were lucky and if she persevered, she might one day be able to sit for an hour a day in a wheelchair. She could hope for nothing more. "It goes along with the whole concept of labeling people, dooming people," she said to me. "The motivation of people is very important and has to be taken into account. It simply wasn't in my case. The doctors more or less said, 'Well, she's paralyzed. So let her go crawl under a rock and wait out her days.'"

She was sent to rehabilitation hospitals. She bucked the doctors. She didn't want to be able to sit for only an hour a day, so during rest periods, she refused to lie down. She struggled mightily to build up stamina. "I wouldn't give in. I just wouldn't give in. I knew it was up to me. I knew no one else was going to help. I was in this alone. I was scared all right, but I was determined." She felt the need to hear encouragement, so she talked to herself. "You can do it, Sandra," she would urge herself. "Those doctors are quacks. You can do it. So do it."

She managed to sit up for well over an hour. When she was discharged from the hospitals, she resumed high school with home instruction. "It was abysmal. Absolutely dreadful. The attitude of the teachers was basically, 'Well, what's the point? What are you going to do with it anyway? Let's just get this over with.'" At length, she got her diploma. Shortly afterward, she was visited by a counselor from the Office of Vocational Rehabilitation. He asked her what she wanted to do. "I was kind of directionless. I had a typewriter with special devices I could use. It was an electric typewriter that used a roll of paper, because I couldn't put paper in. I was already able to sit up for an entire day. I had done some free-lance typing for people, so I asked the counselor about that." He didn't say anything. The counselor fished out a stopwatch to time her. Nervous, she did miserably. He then opened his briefcase and extracted a set of beads and some string. He said he wanted to time her stringing beads.

" 'Forget it,' I told him. I had stopped stringing beads as a child. He blew his stack. He pulled out a kit for putting charms on a bracelet. I refused that. I said I wanted to go to college. He judged me totally uncooperative and stormed out."

Schnur decided she had better do something for herself. She took a proofreading course. Through a friend and innumerable phone calls, she wheedled some free-lance typing and proofreading, and she published several guidebooks for the disabled. "I was lucky that I was determined. My sister once told me that if it had been her, just forget it. She would have become an orange." A year later, Schnur convinced the Vocational Rehabilitation Office to sponsor a college education. Her first year — at Hunter — her father suffered a massive coronary, and Schnur's parents moved to Florida. They wanted her to accompany them, but she refused. She became one of the first severely disabled people to lead an independent life in New York.

"At first, it was living hell. I didn't know how to supervise the attendant I needed. I knew what to tell the person, but I couldn't find the words. I had a block. It's a block a lot of handicapped people know all too well. One of the worst fears that a handicapped person has is that the person caring for him will just up and leave. Say, 'So long, it's been great, but good-bye.' That's exactly what happened to me. Without any notice or anything, she just picked up and left. I was shocked, but I replaced her and gradually I learned to steer the ship."

She gazed out the window. A police car rushed past outside, hurrying to some emergency. Its siren filled the room. One of the windows was only half open. Schnur asked me if I would open the window the rest of the way. I got up and shoved it open.

"When you first find yourself paralyzed," she said, "little

things like realizing that you can't budge that window anymore really get to you. No more. I mean, the window is open.
I had to ask you to do it, but I got it done. That's what you
have to tell yourself — that one way or the other, things will
get done."

After college, Schnur hunted for work. "A lot of employers were nervous and uncomfortable. You can pretty
much sense right away when someone just isn't going to be
able to handle you. One personnel person all but patted me
on the head and said, 'My, how well you drive that chair.'
As if I were a circus act." She eventually found her present
job, with which she is reasonably content. "There's tre-
mendous discrimination in hiring of the handicapped. People
are amazed if we can do anything. You know, look at us
walk. Look at us talk. But we can do almost anything. Just
give us the chance."

A man I'll call Lester Rhome was one of the forty-three
thousand people struck down by the polio epidemic of 1949.
He was left a quadriplegic, and had to be confined to an
iron lung. But he chose not to grieve for himself, and kept
up the feeling that the mere fact of life was miraculous.
He told himself that he had been "forced into a common
denominator by fate," and resolved to make the best of
things. When polio struck, Rhome was thirty-four, married,
and a doctor, with a general medical practice. His own
determination, coupled with strong family support, convinced him to try to take up an aspect of medicine that he
could still practice effectively from the lung. He wrote to
specialists all over the world. A number of suggestions
trickled in. Between refresher courses and actual observation
at a West Coast hospital, he managed to open his practice
again, restricting it to allergy and dermatology disorders.
The field doesn't actually require any physical examination
of the patient, only knowledgeable interpretation based on

sight, symptoms, and listening to the patient's description of the disorder. Then he must map out a course of action with the help of lab tests, prescriptions and follow-up visits. "My limitations don't interfere with my serving my patients one bit," he has said.

Rhome practices his medicine full time from a combination office and home. Patients are already waiting for him when he's wheeled into his office at nine o'clock. He draws about sixty patients a day, the bulk of them coming in for routine allergy injections, lab tests, prescriptions, consultations or diagnostic procedures. Rhome sees all new patients. The patient is positioned on a bench in front of the iron lung, so that Rhome and the patient can view each other in the tilted mirror that is clamped to the lung. One of his two youthful medical assistants crouches beside him, scribbling down notes and the diagnosis. Or else he gently holds a telephone or stethoscope in place. Rhome could not have styled a neater arrangement.

Lester Rhome is living contradiction to the foolish view that the severely handicapped have no place in the work force. "I was told I was pretty much at the end of the road," says Rhome. "I never believed that." He profoundly loves his job. Patients have seemed more friendly than he could have dreamed, and the full warm context of his relationship with them is something wonderful to see. "The children are the best," he remarks. "They keep me honest. They force me to deal with reality, when they put questions to me like: 'Why are you stuck in that big thing?' 'How do you ever get out?' 'Do you have hands and feet?' "

The day's work finished, Rhome is still restless to do things. So he plays chess and poker. He collects antiques and artwork. He is a history buff on the American West. With help from his three full-time attendants, he constructs furniture and ministers to a good-sized garden that is crowded with fruit trees, vegetables, and flowers. In a sense, he is self-reliant beyond the usual meaning of the word.

His life does have complexities. Small things can make a fatal difference. Several years ago, when a storm knocked out the power, the local fire department hastened to his rescue and hand-pumped his iron lung. What's more, he has a direct telephone hook-up to the operator. By flicking his head, a chain attached to his eyeglasses triggers the connection so he can make or receive calls through an intercom speaker system.

When he is at home, he is comforted and easy. Is he bitter? Manifestly not. He is too caught up in what he is doing. Of his life he has much good to say. "I miss things. I miss climbing stairs. I used to play the piano, and I miss that whenever I hear music. But I get great satisfaction from earning my own living. I feel good. I have a healthy respect for my life."

10

On the West Side of Manhattan, not far from the garment district, the Veterans Administration has its Prosthetics Research Center. It is in a gray, hulking building. The problems the handicapped face are substantial, but they would be much worse were it not for technology. For many, independent lives are a possibility only because of the magic of science. The battery of tools now available can help even the most severely handicapped person get through the day without great difficulty. Technology, in effect, is replacing muscles with motors. To find out what was happening in the technological workshop, I paid a visit to the Prosthetics Research Center, a key designer of aids for the handicapped and possibly the most knowledgeable body on what is going on in the field.

The center's director, Anthony Staros, a florid, snowy-haired man, his face alive with wit, took me into his roomy office and told me, "With developments in electronics and microprocessors, and progress in reducing motor sizes and breakthroughs in portable energy storage systems, we see no limit to what can be done to improve the quality of life for the handicapped. What we're doing is trying to make matters better for people who have trouble doing things for themselves. We're getting them out of bed, out of the house, and into offices. We're in effect rescuing them from the living death of uselessness."

Staros pointed out that, because the center is in close contact with VA hospitals spotted around the country that mind a good many disabled patients, it is very much aware of the problems of every imaginable type of disability. "We are unique in this kind of work in that we know what's happening with patients. And we have a ready supply of people on whom to test our inventions."

I asked him what he thought about the state of the art. Just how good a job was research doing to get the handicapped up and about?

He pondered the question a moment, then said, "The state of the art is progressing very nicely and very smoothly and very adequately. I think the state of the field is rather good. Some weak spots remain. Some areas could have been handled better in the past. I think the weakest spot is delivery of service. Our problem is getting the technology to the patient. The patient in Fargo, North Dakota, isn't learning enough about the technology we have. Dissemination of information isn't good. Also, some of the equipment is sophisticated and the people who approve the funds are sitting on them. Once the equipment is available, the funds sometimes aren't there to bring it to the consumer."

Still, Staros was brimming with hope for the future. He said, "I can't even guess at what the limits are. In the next twenty years, I expect to see more and more and more. I wish to hell I were twenty years younger so I could see the things that will be coming down the road."

I was escorted on a tour of several laboratories. The first was the mobility lab. The room was deep in electric wheelchairs. A meaty, ruddy-faced man showed me around. "You can shop for a chair today the way you shop for a car," he said. "We've got all sizes, all sorts of features, a wide price range. Getting a really reliable one that can take a lot of use is a problem. We're always looking for better models."

I was shown the fairly familiar chair that functions by hand controls, another that works by flicking one's chin against a knob. Still another is activated by breath; this was designed for someone who can't even move his head. Two tubes would be adjusted before his mouth. Blowing into both of them moves the chair forward. Inhaling produces reverse. Puffing into the right-hand tube sends the chair to the right; puffing into the left tube turns it left. A particularly rugged model had been designed for outdoor use. It has a heavier frame and smaller, thicker tires with treads. "The difference between this and a regular chair," my escort told me, "is the same as the difference between a jeep and a standard car." I learned about a voice-controlled wheelchair with a computer that responds to voice commands, which activate the necessary controls. Very expensive. Still another chair, I found out, can climb stairs. It features tanklike treads that lock onto stairs. Pressure from the operator's arms against levers causes the chair to ascend or descend along the treads. Its drawback is that the user must have awfully strong muscles.

I was told also of a revolutionary new set of crutches being developed at the University of Houston Mechanical Engineering Department. The wooden pole-vaulting pole has given way to fiberglass, the tennis racket has become metal, but nobody has touched the crutch, the department felt, so it decided to apply "Pogo stick theory" to crutches. Prototypes are being tested that incorporate springs that store energy during part of the motion cycle and then release it in another part. Moving about on crutches requires several times the amount of energy expended in walking without them. The crutches are tricky to get accustomed to, since you need to adopt a swing-through motion, moving both limbs at the same time.

Next, I was shown a breath-activated environmental control system that had been developed by the Veterans Administration for quadriplegics. A model was set up in what amounted to a mock hospital room. A dummy patient lay serenely on a bed sporting slightly soiled sheets. By blowing or sucking on a tube that connects to air switches, the user is able to activate a host of appliances — TV, radio, lamp, alarm clock, air-conditioner, electric door. Even an automatic phone. Blowing into the tube switches on the phone. Numbers begin to flash sequentially on a digital readout; when a desired digit pops up, the user puffs again; he continues puffing at digits until the number is completed. A portable unit that can be mounted on a wheelchair has also been engineered, as has a model that reacts to voice commands. Even breath-activated electric typewriters, I was told, are on the market. A communications system has been invented that enables a severely handicapped person to "draw" an image on a video monitor by eye movement alone. It works with a long-persistence phosphor. The image lasts a couple of minutes, though a video tape recorder can be hooked up to the monitor to record the process for later replay.

"It's quite amazing," the ruddy-faced man said. "You can speak with your eyes. You can move with your mouth. Technology is a wonder."

Carl Mason, a fast-talking, bespectacled man, whisked me through the advanced systems lab, of which he is head. "I will show you things that will blow your mind and make your eyes pop out of your head," he promised. First he showed me a videotape of a patient testing an experimental "quadriplegic manipulator." Two small analog computers drive the device, which is basically a steel arm with a hook at the end, mounted on a wheelchair. "What we're trying to do," Mason said, "is develop, in effect, a third arm for quadriplegics." The user controls the device with his or her chin. On the screen, the patient was using the arm to snatch up a fork and feed himself, to hoist a briefcase, to fetch a glass of water, even to play a game of chess. (He made some good moves.) Mason said that the arm can move at speeds between a millimeter a second and a meter a second. He said the manipulator will need testing and evaluation for another three to five years. "We've been working on it for some time," he said. "A lot of sweat and blood went into that metal arm. We haven't found any major bugs so far. We're very hopeful."

Mason next showed me a myoelectric hand, which is already being used. People who lose hands still retain the two sets of muscles in the arm that drive the hand, and so electrodes can be attached to these muscles that are, in turn, hooked to an electric hand. Flexing the arm muscles directs the fake hand to open and close as if it were the real thing. It responds just as quickly as a real hand, Mason said. A few hundred people already wear myoelectric hands; even more probably would, Mason pointed out, except that it retails for about seven hundred dollars: "A lot to cough up for a hand." Mason had a demonstration myoelectric hand rigged up to some electrodes that he connected to his own arm, and he invited me to shake hands with it. It was like shaking hands with Godzilla.

"You expected some sissy handshake, now didn't you?" Mason said. He paused to chuckle, to flash a grin. "This hand can really shake, boy."

As I wiggled my hand to rid it of numbness, Mason said, "The next stage is to allow the user to feel what is happening with the hand. Now he can tell only by looking at it. He could be strangling you and not know it if he were looking elsewhere. We don't want these hands locked up, now do we? We don't yet know how to give exactly the same feeling. The user will be able to sense the amount of force, though, if our current development work succeeds. He won't feel temperature. You can stick a hot poker in the hand and he won't notice anything. The aim is to give a person control so he won't pick up a vase to admire it and shatter it into a million pieces, or he won't grab his martini too lightly and spill it on some lady's dress."

Mason hopped onto a contraption that resembled a wheelchair, except that one stands up on it. He flicked a switch and started whirling around the room. At one point, he spun around several times, like a ballet dancer doing pirouettes. Buckles kept him from tumbling out of the device. Called a para-ambulation platform, the thing is designed for indoor use by paraplegics, so they can grab things off shelves and perform tasks they couldn't accomplish in a wheelchair. The platform moves on drive carriages, tiny wheels mounted at angles in a circle, similar to airport luggage conveyors. It moves at a speed of a mile and a half per hour, Mason said, and can stop on a dime. It's weighted so it won't tip over.

"Watch me," Mason said, and he punched the throttle and bounded toward a counter, against which two lab men were leaning.

"Uh-oh," one of the men said. "Here comes the mad scientist. Everybody duck."

The men dived behind the counter, but didn't need to. As Mason rumbled to within an inch of it, he hit another button and the thing stopped.

"So you see," Mason said, "you don't have to worry about someone coming into your house with one of these and sending chairs and bookcases flying." The system is still experimental and won't be ready for routine patient use for some time.

I dropped in next on Howard Freiberger, an electronics engineer whose specialty is sensory devices for the blind. He told me about the Bionic Laser Cane, which shoots out thin beams of laser light in three directions to detect drop-offs, straight-ahead obstacles and objects rising between the chest and head. When the beams sense something, the traveler is warned through auditory and tactile signals. The cane's limitations are that it can't "see" through glass, and heavy rain or snow will sometimes trigger false alarms. Then Freiberger described the Sonicguide, which was inspired by the way bats flit about. This, a transmitter housed in a pair of lightweight eyeglass frames, emits ultrasonic sound waves. When the waves hit an object and bounce back, receivers in the glasses transform them into audible sounds. The sounds are transmitted through small tubes into the user's ears. Since it only works on objects at least waist-high, the Sonicguide must be used in conjunction with a cane or dog.

"These devices can be considerably improved upon," Freiberger said. "They do what they're supposed to do, but they work well for some people, not so well for others. They take quite a bit of getting used to. We have hopes for much better aids."

Freiberger also told me about the Optacon, a reading device that has been around for several years. It converts print into a vibrating, tactile form. The blind person eases a pocketknife-sized camera across a line of print with one hand. The index finger of the other hand is placed on a special board. As the camera picks up a letter, the image is simultaneously reproduced on the board by miniature vibrating rods, which the "reading" finger feels. A lot of training is needed to get used to the Optacon, Freiberger said. Some particularly facile blind people, however, can read as many as seventy words a minute with it. Another, newer device, Freiberger said, is the Kurzweil Reading Machine, which scans a printed page and turns print into audible synthetic speech. It employs a minicomputer that can read most typestyles and can store an extensive vocabulary. Freiberger didn't happen to have a machine handy (which didn't surprise me, since they sell for roughly fifty thousand dollars), but he played me a tape of a machine's performance. Before he flicked it on, he handed me a printed copy of the text of the machine's assignment. The voice was deep and sounded like a record being played at one speed too slow. Some of the reading was intelligible enough, though certain words and passages were garbled and all but impossible to understand.

"It's the best of this kind so far," Freiberger said. "It's a variety that has generated a lot of interest. We're just not sure yet if a much better model can be developed. We all hope so."

For deaf people, aside from the limited and costly TTYs, I learned eventually, HC Electronics of Mill Valley, California, has come up with a hand-held, battery-operated electronic voice system that allows both deaf people and mute people to communicate with hearing people. Known as the Phonic Mirror Handi Voice, it can (according to the company) parrot the human voice, utter complete sentences, and speak almost every word in the English language. The product makes use of forty-five phonemes, or basic sound elements, in a variety of combinations to simulate the human voice electronically. A person presses numerical codes on the keyboard, and a voice wafts from a built-in speaker. The voice is deep, nasal and machinelike, on the order of a talking computer. The artificial voice sells for around two thousand dollars. It's still too soon to judge its effectiveness.

The American Humane Association in Denver has started a program to train dogs to help the deaf in much the same manner that Seeing Eye dogs assist the blind. The dogs are taught to scamper between a sound and the owner until the person realizes something is up. Also, they are custom-trained for special purposes. One owner, for instance, requested that his dog learn to pick up anything that falls out of his pockets. He had lost two wallets because he never heard them drop.

Elsewhere on the animal front, at the New England Medical Center Hospital, Dr. M. J. Willard is training monkeys to act as personal aides for quadriplegics. What is eventually sought is a network of monkey-helper training centers. Thus far, four monkeys are undergoing schooling. Each is a capuchin monkey, commonly known as the organ-grinder monkey, which has a reputation for being smart and docile. The first monkey, named Crystel, is expected to graduate shortly, after a year and a half of training. She has been serving a quadriplegic who lives in a residence hotel in Boston. The goal of the program is not to supplant human attendants. Crystel can't lift her owner out of bed or dress or bathe him. However, she can free him from some of the metes and bounds of his disability. Crystel has learned to open and close doors, turn lights on and off, put records on a phonograph and fetch small items like keys or books when a light beam is shone on them. What's more, she can feed him simple foods like applesauce or porridge. At present, I was told by Dr. Willard, about ninety-five percent of the food gets in her owner, five percent on her owner. Dr. Willard is still working at teaching Crystel to escort her owner to the supermarket and place items in a bag on the back of the wheelchair. Training has, for the most part, proceeded with considerable success, Dr. Willard informed me. Mishaps have been held to a minimum. Early on, Crystel, who lives in the shower of the hotel room, presumably got miffed at something or other and draped toilet paper throughout the bathroom. In addition, she left the water running in the sink until it had seeped down through two floors of the hotel. She is now behaving better.

Some weeks later, I paid a visit to what's been dubbed "the world's largest unknown organization." The organization is the Telephone Pioneers of America. Always publicity shy, the Pioneers boast some 510,000 members, hailing from every state and Canada. Eligibility requires at least eighteen years of service at the American Telephone and Telegraph Company. In some respects, the Pioneers is a fraternal organization that applies some of the same sorts of balm to social needs as does, say, the Elks or Moose. However, a good chunk of Pioneers' time over the last couple of decades has been spent inventing a stunning array of devices to improve the lives of the handicapped.

One brisk, windy day I called on the national secretary of the Pioneers, a hefty, bespectacled fellow with an egg-shaped face named Stanley Blauser. He's an uncommonly genial individual, with a big booming voice, who seems to have been born to head a fraternal organization. His office is at 22 Cortlandt Street, deep in the heart of Lower Manhattan, where telephone company offices squat on the offices of *The Wall Street Journal,* which squat on Woolworth's. When I came in, Blauser stuck out a hand and said, "It's great to meet you. Just sit wherever is comfortable. Take my chair, if that's best."

After fetching me some coffee, Blauser began by rattling off some Pioneers background. The organization was founded in 1911, with Alexander Graham Bell installed as the first member. "We started mainly as a social organization. The idea was to establish a formal, personal tie for the older employees with the company from which they were likely to retire." In the 1950s, the organization decided that socializing was fun and all, but the world had a lot of problems. "The telephone business, you see, is a very service-oriented industry," Blauser explained, "so telephone company employees have service in their blood. At least they do after they've worked here eighteen years. So we wanted to pitch in and help. In 1958, we formally made it part of our charter to do community projects. We build parks and restore landmark buildings, but the biggest emphasis has been on helping the handicapped. That just seemed like a good cause, and our interest was helped by the fact that Alexander Graham Bell was a teacher of the deaf." Since 1958, the Pioneers has conceived no less than three hundred aids for people with disabilities. Members undertake the work on their own time, often out of basement workshops.

"We're not necessarily inventing electricity," Blauser pointed out. "In most cases, we're coming up with shrewd adaptations of existing things."

Blauser excused himself for a moment, and he scuffled into another room. He returned with his arms brimming with an assortment of contraptions. "Here's my bag of tricks," he boomed.

He set his armload crashing down onto the desk. Thumbing through the devices, he picked out a Wilson king-sized softball. Except for being larger, it looked like any old softball kids might beat around the schoolyard. "This is one of our great inventions," Blauser said proudly. "The beep baseball."

Fifteen years ago, Ina Guyer, a Mountain Bell employee, looked on sympathetically as a blind child in Colorado Springs stumbled and groped to find a ball in a field. The idea of a beeping softball sprang into being. A telephone engineer in Denver assembled an experimental ball with an electronic beeper and amplifier buried inside. Then San Francisco Pioneers took the idea still further. They engineered beeping cone-shaped bases and a fan-shaped field. The blind could play ball.

Blauser pulled a lever on the side of the ball, like a pin on a hand grenade, and the ball began to give off a high-pitched and continuous *beep-beep-beep*. Wilson Sporting Goods makes the actual balls, then the Pioneers hollow them out and stick in the beeping devices. The balls are then sold at cost to blind people. Around six thousand are pounded out every year. One of the first beep balls now reposes in the Baseball Hall of Fame.

"The nature of beep baseball has changed dramatically," Blauser said. "It was originally designed as therapy for kids. Now it's become competitive. We've got adults playing beep baseball. In fact, we have several former professional athletes who lost their sight who are playing the game. Boy, they hit that ball with a wallop. The earlier balls we made are useless. The hides would get ripped off. We've had to design a much sturdier version."

Beep basketball was conceived by West Virginia Pioneers. A ball laced with bells is shot against a backboard wired for sound. The St. Lawrence, Canada, chapter came up with an audible hockey puck. A beeping horseshoe game was invented by an Alabama member. A beeping putting device for blind golfers came out of the San Diego chapter. A New York Telephone switchman invented a bowling aid that uses lights and raised prongs on a panel to allow a visually impaired bowler to know what pins remain standing.

Blauser showed me a cricket. It looks like a small telescope with a clamp attached to it. It was designed to fit on the back of a bike pedaled by a sighted person. Flick on a switch and it starts to beep. A blind person on a trailing bike can follow the sound and therefore be able to ride a bicycle.

Next, Blauser held up a big chart headed, "Feeling for Color." "A lot of blind people have trouble matching colors," he explained. "If no one was around to help them, they'd go out looking like a horror show. Here's the solution." Ten small patches of different colors — green, gray, red, tan, blue, etc. — were affixed to the chart, with braille letters embossed on them. They could be sewn on clothing of the appropriate color so a blind person could know what he was putting on.

I was shown a magnetic finger. A dowel stick having a cylindrical magnet glued to its end will attract an ordinary paper clip pushed onto the edge of the page of a book or magazine. If clips are staggered on adjacent pages, they can be turned by a slow horizontal arm movement. Thus the magnetic finger allows people with slight arm, hand, and finger control to flip pages and read without help.

"We've recently come up with a really exciting development," Blauser said. "Statistics say that two or three babies out of every hundred have some sort of hearing impairment at birth. If you don't catch it early, the hearing deteriorates and the baby may go deaf or may never be able to learn to talk. One of the biggest problems is detecting hearing impairments early. The Pioneers out on the West Coast have been working for years with a doctor, whom they hired, to design and build a small machine that can be carried around to hospitals and people's homes to give a brain stem evoke response test. The test isn't new, but the machines to perform it are mammoth, taking up a whole room, and cost maybe thirty thousand dollars. Not many hospitals have them. The machine we developed is portable and costs about a thousand dollars to build. Our ultimate objective is to test every baby that's born at birth. That's a tall order, but we think big around here."

Blauser leaned back in his chair and reflected on what else he might have left out. His eyes suddenly lit up. "I'll tell you something else," he said. "We have clown schools. Our members go to them and learn clown stunts and magic tricks. Then we go around to homes for invalids and to rehabilitation centers and entertain. We've set up blind nature trails across the country. Basically, all you do is carve out a trail, then at various junctures you install a tape recorder in a tree or something that tells you about the animals and plants there. Something else we're proud of is that our local chapters try to round up lists of disabled people in the area who are homebound. We send them birthday cards. We visit them. We throw little parties for them. Whatever we can do to show them someone cares."

11

W HEREVER I went, I asked people what they thought was the key to the discrimination puzzle. In every instance, they immediately said, "Attitudes." One after the other, people told me that if attitudes were to change, everything else would neatly fall into place. I determined to find out more about why attitudes were what they were and what could be done about them by checking with the professionals. Over the years, I learned, voluminous research has grown up around attitudes toward the handicapped and attitudes of the handicapped toward themselves. I had no trouble finding explanations for why people react as they do toward the disabled. Indeed, I found a grab bag of competing and often contradictory explanations — some of which bore a suspicious resemblance to old wives' tales I had heard. But the first and possibly the most significant thing I learned was that nothing about attitudes toward the handicapped is as simple as it seems — for the reason that nothing about any attitudes is as simple as it seems.

The biggest name in the attitude field — the first one to come up in any discussion of the topic — is Harold Yuker. Early on a raw Monday evening, Yuker came sidling across the bar of Hofstra's University Club as if he owned the place.

He might just as well own the place. He had recently been promoted to provost of Hofstra. He had the look of someone who knows he is eagerly anticipated. In his mid-fifties, he looked dapper in a gray flannel sport jacket, a white shirt, and a red-and-green bowtie. The limp from the cerebral palsy he has lived with all his life was pronounced.

"Come over, come over, come over," he said. We ordered drinks and then Yuker led me to a table. He walked slowly, jerkily, as though each step were painful.

We sat down at an uncluttered table in the corner of the room. Several people huddled around the horseshoe bar, not talking about much. Two of them were giggling over some tidbit of gossip. In response to my first question, Yuker said, "Attitudes toward the handicapped are very bad. Very bad. Studies show that only a bit more than half of the population of the United States expresses slightly positive attitudes toward the disabled. The rest openly admit to negative attitudes. They see the handicapped as different and in some ways inferior to normal people. They are terribly uncomfortable in their presence. They would like to see the handicapped segregated, perhaps locked away in glass bottles. To make it as a disabled person, you must be prepared for great difficulties and privation. The discrimination is just searing. Fainthearted disabled people never escape from their cocoons."

Yuker told me that he never had any idea he would become the authority on attitudes toward the handicapped. In 1956, he was contentedly teaching psychology at Hofstra, when a place called Abilities Incorporated asked him to do some part-time research into the problems of disability. At the time, he had had virtually no contact with other handicapped people, and had nourished the myopic view that he really wasn't handicapped. However, Abilities Incorporated intrigued him. It was begun in 1952 by a man named Henry Viscardi. Born without legs, he decided to start a factory employing only the disabled to encourage the idea that they were capable workers. The factory was turning out to everyone's satisfaction, but unfortunately it wasn't enjoying anywhere near the impact staked out for it. Frustrated, Viscardi figured he needed research — cold facts — to trumpet to the world. Yuker was mentioned to him as the man to get the facts. "Frankly, I was very troubled about being thrust into the world of the disabled, a world I had always denied being part of," Yuker said. "But then again, it was a real challenge." The challenge flushed Yuker into action.

By no means had Yuker been free of discrimination. While he was a graduate student, he was bluntly told time and again by his professors that he could forget about getting a teaching job with his disability. He was told (and he still believes this to be the case) that he would never find a teaching job in New York City, because of his speech. His voice is slow and choppy, as if from fatigue. Yuker would parry any such opinion or comment with one standard remark: "Oh be quiet. You don't know what you're talking about." Since he started teaching, Yuker has found that a certain percentage of students drop out of his courses because they don't care to learn from a cripple.

Interrupting his teaching, Yuker undertook a couple of studies and discovered that attitudes clearly were critical to the whole problem of disability, both the attitudes of the able-bodied toward the disabled, and also the attitudes of the disabled toward themselves. He found that if a handicapped person emphasized his limitations, he did poorly on the job. But if he stressed his remaining abilities, he did well.

Distraught that research done so far in the field was sketchy and inadequate, Yuker resolved to come up with some sort of grand scale to measure attitudes toward the disabled. He spent eight years developing it. In 1966, he at last published a monograph that laid out his Attitudes Toward Disabled Persons Scale. It has become the most-used test in the world in this field. Yuker knows of its involvement in more than four hundred studies. He hit on the scale by testing some two hundred items that appeared to be particularly relevant to a person's attitudes about disability. He weeded out less pertinent ones until the number eventually settled down to thirty items. Using the scale, he canvassed all manner of individuals — students, employers, employees — and found a striking correlation in their response. "Attitudes were bad, and bad across all disabilities. We were as anonymous as so many plastic spoons." Surprising findings turned up. His work indicated that, regardless of whether someone was born disabled or acquired his handicap, he felt the same about himself. (The prevailing theory held that if you're born with a disability, you can more easily accustom yourself to it.) Another startling finding was that the severity of the disability didn't matter: someone minus an arm wasn't any better adjusted to his situation than a bedridden quadriplegic. That went smack against previous assumption.

Given that attitudes are bad, what can be done about it? I asked Yuker.

"We don't really know how to change attitudes," he answered. "Changing attitudes is one of the most befuddling things that confronts us. We have good evidence that attitudes of nondisabled people change when contact is made with a disabled person superior to them. But most people, as you know, never come into contact with a disabled person superior to them. We have no badge of respectability. When I give a speech, people are impressed by my position, my success. I'm a big shot. But most people don't come into contact with me, or people like me. You know, if we came over from the bar to here, I'd have to ask you to carry my drink, because my hands just aren't steady enough. I've dropped more drinks than I care to remember. About once a year, I do ask someone to carry my drink who doesn't know me. They invariably say, 'What's the matter, are you crippled or something?' They're terribly embarrassed when they find out I am."

Yuker gave a short, brusque laugh. The laugh started his eyebrows and the corners of his mouth dancing. He said, "You can really feel the impact of your presence in a room. You come in and everybody has feelings about you. It's like iron filings standing on end in the presence of a magnet. When you leave, the room demagnetizes."

Mainstreaming, Yuker said, would undoubtedly do some good. "I've been arguing for this for twenty years. I've yelled and shouted and banged my fist. We have been in this incredible bureaucratic holding pattern. You've got to get everybody together at an early age, before people start to notice differences."

"That's a slow solution," I said.

He grinned like a Cheshire cat. "Attitudes always change slowly," he said. "This is the same with blacks and women and Puerto Ricans. No magic pills can be taken. No surgery can be performed. Only time does it."

What about handicapped people now looking for jobs and places to live? I said.

"The solution is to say that this is the law and you better comply," Yuker said. "Pressure, in other words. I think the handicapped population must become more militant. I think the problem is that the disabled issue is on the back burner. Bureaucrats are dawdling. I'm very disturbed that many disabled people are working with other disabled people, rather than working in the able-bodied world. In part, it's because it's easier. I learned early in my career that in order for me to get a job I'd have to be a hell of a lot better than the others applying for that job. And I don't think the world has changed that much since. The handicapped have got to light the fuse."

I asked Yuker what he thought would improve quickest, the attitudes of the nondisabled toward the disabled or the attitudes of the disabled toward themselves.

He said, "I think the problem of changing the attitudes of disabled people will be the harder nut to crack. They have lived their lives feeling like doormats. That's going to be very, very hard to change. A lot of it, of course, has to do with how you were brought up. See, when I was a kid my parents never did a damn thing for me. They made me do everything myself, no matter how much I whined. And I was pretty good at whining. Do this. Do that. If they hadn't been like that, if they had waited on me, I'd hate to think of where I'd be today. Probably stitching wallets in a sheltered workshop."

I went to see Robert Kleck. A talkative, hospitable man with a smooth manner and a modish style, Kleck is a psychologist at Dartmouth College. The biggest chunk of his work has had to do with the study of handicapped behavior. When I got in touch with him and asked him about the state of the field, he said, "A lot of work has been of dubious validity and believability. A lot of research has been done, but you have to be awfully careful with it."

Kleck himself joined the field somewhat accidentally. While working toward his Ph.D. at Stanford, he studied under a professor with a strong interest in the disabled. Kleck began to dabble in the subject, and liked it enough to stick with it full time. Kleck isn't disabled at all, nor did he have any exposure to the handicapped growing up, which is somewhat unusual for a specialist in this field.

"You will find many people in this area who are handicapped, have handicapped children or parents, or are good friends with some handicapped person," he said. "A personal curiosity prods a lot of researchers, and at times their bias can be too powerful." Kleck paused a moment (we were talking on the phone), then hastily put in, "I should tell you, though, that I'm tall. Really tall. Six-foot-six. I grew up in Ohio, and between the ages of fourteen and twenty-one, all encounters between me and other males began, 'Who do you play basketball for?' So I know something about the social problems of unusual appearance."

Investigators into handicaps, broadly speaking, split up into two camps. One camp feels that attitudes trigger behavior, the other camp that behavior shapes attitudes. Kleck is a behavior man. He told me, "In my opinion, behavior, not attitude, is the problem. In my view, attitude follows behavior. I tend to downplay attitude. Others say it's everything."

Kleck brought up one of his most revealing experiments. He recruited forty-six juniors from a local high school to take part in what he called a "psychological study." He didn't tell the subjects that the experiment had anything to do with the handicapped. Instead, he explained that the point of the study was to look at people's physiological reactions during face-to-face encounters. Subjects arrived individually, and electrodes were affixed to one of the person's hands to measure general physiological activity. Around five minutes later, the other party would rap on the door. In some cases, he was a perfectly normal person who strode in and shook hands. In other instances, he was missing a leg and clacked in in a wheelchair. Dummy electrodes were also attached to the second party, so the true subject wouldn't get suspicious of what was going on. Nothing was said about his disability. The subject was always asked to do the interviewing. The amputee was given five questions, told to ask them and then take notes on a clipboard. The questions went: What do you consider important in forming impressions on others? How important is academic achievement in high schools? How important are sports in school? How important is religion in a person's life? How important is physical appearance in the impressions you form of others? After the interviewer left, Kleck asked a few additional questions to get the subject's impressions of the other person and his reaction to the situation.

"It was very easy to demonstrate that behavior is affected in a number of pretty significant ways, depending on who is doing the interviewing," Kleck told me. "You could tell right away, just from the face of the subject, if he was talking to a normal person or a handicapped person. If it was a handicapped person, the subject's palms tended to sweat, his heart beat faster, he was nervous, and his body moved less freely. Another thing was that a person didn't get as physically close to a handicapped person, and if he had the option, he would terminate the interaction much faster than normal. Also, the opinions that were expressed to the handicapped person were often changed considerably from what the subject in truth believed. The subject would always try to say what he felt would be most agreeable to this poor handicapped fellow. For instance, he would always say academic achievement was important in school. Sports were not, even if the guy happened to be captain of the football team and was on the verge of flunking out. He would always say that physical appearance didn't matter one bit. This really isn't a very positive way to handle the situation. All it does is tend to make the handicapped person become overly sure of his reality, which works mightily to his disadvantage."

In a different study, Kleck asked people to rate subjects

on how well they performed a task — such as a paper-folding exercise — and how much motivation they seemed to have. Both handicapped and normal subjects were again used. "People said that performance was equal between handicapped and nonhandicapped individuals, but the handicapped person was more motivated," Kleck said. "In other words, we think the handicapped person must be more motivated to do an average performance. Or else we think unusual skill is involved. All this speaks to the stereotype that the disabled person is less able to perform tasks."

Kleck has done a lot of work looking at social relationships between children with and without handicaps, after they have had some time to get to know one another. His aim has been to see if long exposure changes behavior. As subjects, he chose almost two hundred nine- to fourteen-year-old boys attending Fresh Air Fund summer camps in New York State. Half were handicapped, half were not. At camp's end, the boys were questioned about their impressions of their campmates. Even after several weeks together in pleasant surroundings, the visibly handicapped boys were least preferred, the nonvisibly handicapped boys filled an intermediate position, and the nonhandicapped boys were liked best. "The worst thing you could be," Kleck said, "is physically disabled and physically unattractive. Then you're at the absolute bottom of the social totem pole." Kleck plans next to examine friendship formation among handicapped kids. "Some researchers maintain that those who choose friends who are disabled are people who have low social credit themselves. But we don't have enough data on this."

I asked Kleck what the solutions were.

He said, "The legislation that will make disabled people visible — in schools, in buses, in apartment buildings — will bring some good with more contact. One thing my research tells me is that frequency of contact improves our comfort with handicapped people." He added that a lot depends on a handicapped person's ability to handle what he labels the "attribution dilemma." Does he blame the way people act toward him on his handicap, or on the rest of his personality and appearance? Kleck said that some people use their disability as a crutch to explain away why others don't like them. But some, he said, deal with the dilemma so well that others respond to them as if nothing at all were wrong with them. "The thing I haven't figured out," Kleck added, "is how handicapped people accomplish this. That's going to take some digging."

The last expert I talked to was Jerome Siller, a professor of education psychology at New York University's School of Education, who has been hard at work in the field since 1956. He is a burly man. Stocky. His hair is thick but graying. A serious turn of mind. When I called on him, the first thing he said was, "Research has told us that the public believes the disabled are different, and the way society is constituted we tend to hold people who are different in a negative fashion. Many individuals believe that handicapped people are strange and frightening."

Much of Siller's work has dealt with how able-bodied people react to specific disabilities. One of the key tools his research has yielded is a series of measures of people's attitudes known as Disability Factor Scales. They are similar to Harold Yuker's scale, though Yuker's measures attitudes toward the disabled in general, while Siller's are more concerned with attitudes toward particular handicaps. The scales measure things like "interaction strain" and "rejection of intimacy" and "imputed functional limitations."

Use of Siller's scales had produced a sort of disability hierarchy. The most acceptable class of handicaps, he found, are those that are relatively minor, such as partial loss of vision, a speech impediment, some loss of hearing, a heart condition. Next in acceptability are those who have lost a limb, who are helped by the fact that an artificial arm or leg makes their injury barely noticeable. The blind and deaf fall into a middle category (even though loss of sight or hearing are almost invariably dreaded as the worst handicaps to suffer). Then come people who are mentally ill. At the bottom of the acceptability ladder are those with acute brain or muscular impairments, such as epilepsy, cerebral palsy, total paralysis. Oddly enough, the worst attitudes are often directed at the obese. "This has been confirmed in a number of studies," Siller said to me. "We simply don't like the fat."

Siller told me that John Tringo, a psychologist at the University of Kentucky, asked a large group of students and rehabilitation workers to rank twenty-one different disabilities in order of acceptability. His results, in order of tolerance: ulcer, arthritis, asthma, diabetes, heart disease, amputee, blindness, deafness, stroke, cancer, old age, paraplegic, epilepsy, dwarf, cerebral palsy, hunchback, tuberculosis, exconvict, mental retardation, alcoholism, and mental illness.

More than most researchers, Siller has tried to get at why the able-bodied react as they do to the handicapped. He rattled off a batch of possibilities. Pure aesthetic repulsion, he said, appeared to be a common cause. We are taught from childhood on, and ads reinforce, that beautiful is desirable. "Why else all these stupid beauty contests? Why else plaster these billboards with the most striking faces?" Further, most people haven't been exposed to anybody handicapped, and are therefore unsure how they ought to behave around someone who's disabled. Also, the able-bodied people fear becoming disabled themselves. The handicapped, Siller said, act as a reminder of what can happen to any of us. "Just as many people don't like to visit hospitals because they don't want to be reminded of sickness, many shun the disabled for the very same reason. Someone in a wheelchair says to them that one day they, too, might be sitting in a wheelchair." A lot of people, Siller said, feel guilty about being able-bodied while they're around the handicapped. "They wonder why they got such a good shake of the dice." Moreover, Siller says, some people seriously believe that disability is a punishment, and that, consequently, a disabled person is both evil and dangerous. Literature and folklore haven't helped much. Hunchbacks, and men with hooks for hands or pegs for legs are often depicted as wicked. "I should hasten to mention," Siller said, "that a small group of individuals believe somewhat the opposite. A few very religious people I chatted with think that the disabled are to be awed, because they have been specifically selected by God as martyrs who must suffer tribulations in order to prove that God has the power to punish the rest of us for our sins. In other words, the disabled are a symbol of God's wrath. I must admit that this isn't a terribly popular view."

One question that deserves more study, Siller said, was the matter of how much the disabled contribute to the strain felt by the able-bodied by being different. "For instance," he said, "blind people have gestures or movements known as 'blindisms.' When blind people talk with you, they often close their eyes or make queer facial expressions. That certainly doesn't put a sighted person at ease."

And solutions?

Siller said, "Well, we've got to get the disabled to improve their perceptions of themselves. We need to have them say, 'Hey, what the hell am I ashamed for? Other people's limitations are the problem.' A good bit of clinical experience suggests that the way the disabled perceive themselves has a strong effect on the attitudes of others. We need more interaction, that's for sure. But the nature of the interaction is important. If your experience with a disabled person is with a blind beggar on the street, the effect of the interaction will be quite a bit different from your interaction with a corporation executive in his fancy office. That's why blind beggars do a vast disservice to the handicapped, and that's why I would never give any money to those chaps."

Angry at their dreary public image, the more militant handicapped groups have started to gnash their teeth and lash out at some improbable targets. They have, for example, accused some of the traditional service organizations like the March of Dimes, Easter Seal, and the American Foundation for the Blind of, in effect, picturing them as objects of pity. They have pestered these groups to stop using doleful-looking children in braces on fund-raising posters and telethons. To call attention to their grievances, in early 1977 two dozen people in wheelchairs demonstrated at the United Cerebral Palsy Telethon in New York, because, as one demonstrator put it, "They portray us as poor helpless cripples. But we grow up, and a lot of us work, keep house, and make love." The handicapped have had sharp words for Jerry Lewis, long-time king of the muscular dystrophy telethon. One disabled Californian told me, "Some people think Jerry Lewis is God. I think he does as much damage as good. Why not have a let's-plan-for-the-future approach to fund-raising, rather than a poor, helpless approach?" As a matter of fact, a doctoral candidate in psychology at Indiana University did a dissertation on the workings of telethons a few years ago. He came to the conclusion that just as much money would come rolling in if an upbeat tack were tried.

"I have never seen someone in a wheelchair on a quiz show," one blustery, blunt handicapped person said to me one day as we were driving down a midwestern highway. "I think wheelchair users would be great for floor wax commercials, because our wheelchairs scuff up floors like crazy. Why not have a police dispatcher on Adam 12 be a guy in a wheelchair? Why not, when they take a sample to the lab, have the lab guy walk with a limp? Let's have some realism."

The successful television police drama, *Ironsides,* starred Raymond Burr as a paraplegic detective. Most disabled people, though, found the show counterproductive. "I can't see the police setting up something like that," a wheelchair user told me. "In every episode, two or three instances would make a person in a wheelchair laugh. The doors were always wide enough for Ironsides. Not once did he get hopelessly wedged in a door. He could always – and I mean always – find a place to park right outside where he was going. He never had a problem finding curb cuts so he could cross the street. The show was beneficial in the sense that it showed someone in a wheelchair coping with everyday life. But it gave such a distorted image. The producers could have had Ironsides do a great many things that paraplegics are capable of. For example, you can dance in a wheelchair. I have a lot of friends who balance on their back two wheels and boogie with the best of them. When you reach a curb, you can tip back your wheels and charge the curb. Of course you need time to learn these things and you better practice with a football helmet on."

Another handicapped person told me that a friend of his had written to Norman Lear to persuade him to allow Meathead on *All in the Family* to bring home somebody in a wheelchair. After all, he had brought home virtually everything else. Lear wrote back that the topic was too hot for Archie Bunker to handle.

The entire advertising community has pretty much remained removed and aloof from the disabled. The couple of exceptions, though, have been striking. Several years ago,

Chase Manhattan Bank did a string of ten-second TV spots that included an actor in the role of a computer programmer. He sat in a wheelchair, and nothing was said about it. The commercial was the result of heavy pressure on ad agencies from handicapped groups. In a recent issue of *New West* magazine, I spotted a half-page ad for "Paz," a bed and bath shop located in Berkeley. The ad featured a backdrop of shower curtains, and a lone woman seated in a motorized wheelchair in the foreground. She was nattily dressed. She was smiling.

12

In the nation's capital.

The headquarters of the Office for Civil Rights is down a labyrinth of twisted corridors in the fortresslike gull-gray HEW building on Independence Avenue. In the ground-floor government bookstore are half a dozen books explaining the rights of the handicapped people under the law, and lengthy lists of agencies that they can turn to for help. More information is available at the civil-rights office upstairs. The office is the principal enforcer, the last arbitrator short of the courts, of the vast Rehabilitation Act. (It has caretaker responsibility for the compliance of the many thousands of recipients of HEW funds. Most other federal agencies are still, six years after the passage of the law, in the process of writing their own regulations; when they get them done, they must enforce them.) Most discrimination complaints eventually find their way to a civil-rights regional office, where, sooner or later, they are looked into.

The office is trying hard to set things right. Obviously, it wants to. Its people speak with mounting enthusiasm. Checks will be made. The problems will be clarified and addressed. But, of course, difficulties remain. In general, some of the strongest barriers to quicker, better compliance appear to lie within the government itself. Budget limitations have kept the handicapped crew small, and the group is often uncertain how best to spend its time and money. People in the office talk about working twenty-hour days. They admit that they aren't able to monitor properly even their existing sheaf of complaints. The office has never been very efficient in disposing of discrimination complaints brought by blacks and women. The new law is quite a burden to place on the civil-rights office's finite resources.

I called on Jim Bennett, the head of a newly formed technical assistance unit, set up in 1977 to help federal recipients comply voluntarily with the regulations of the Rehabilitation Act. On the door to his office was a sign that said, "Know your rights as a disabled person. 'No qualified person shall on the basis of handicap be subject to discrimination.'" On his desk, sheets of paper were scattered all about. A mug of tea was at his right hand. Bennett greeted me in the somewhat strained if friendly manner of someone who had too often played host to visitors with angry opinions. Bennett is big, open-faced, his sandy hair plastered down on his head, with piercing eyes and big active hands. He has a narrow mustache and his chin juts out forcefully. He sits in a wheelchair (he's postpolio). But if you forget that, he is so clean-cut he looks like a Marine recruiter. Yet he has stormy ideas in his head.

"Part of the reason we are where we are now," Bennett said to me, "is the government's approach to the handicapped. It has historically felt that the handicapped needed separate agencies. Increasingly, it has catered to them in small, special agencies. The fact that this has not worked is proved by the plight most handicapped people find themselves in now. The highest unemployment level. The lowest education level. Jobs that are the least profitable. So now the tack is to have larger, specialized agencies where handicapped people would have a special department. I think this is much worse. The solution is to destroy super agencies to the fullest extent possible and to make services available to the handicapped from the same agencies that handle people in general. Instead of having a counselor for handicapped people, have the same counselor for regular people counsel handicapped people. Instead of a rehabilitation hospital, have all hospitals be capable of handling the handicapped. This won't work for all disabled people, but it will for a great many. We hope this is what the law will accomplish."

But how soon can the handicapped get what they want? What is the real potential for compliance? The civil-rights office employs 1,100 people. An application sits before Congress to boost staffing by 898 workers, because of the thick backlog of complaints. Some three thousand complaints are on file, a number of them going back years, that have yet to be investigated. Because matters were taking so long, rules were laid down in 1977 that the office must investigate cases within ninety days. After that, it has thirty days to attempt to negotiate a solution before turning to the courts. The penalty for someone found guilty of noncompliance is a loss of federal funds, something HEW hasn't yet resorted to. Discrimination complaints in the handicapped area, Bennett told me, did not begin until 1974, when seven were filed. Since then, they have come on strong, thanks to a better awareness by the disabled population of its rights. The totals were 36 in 1975, 117 in 1976, 541 in 1977, and about 1,500 in 1978. Less than half of them have been resolved. The statistics are depressing. I was uncomfortably aware that Bennett and his people live with them every day. "We are busting people's asses to get those cases closed," Bennett told me. "But you can do only so much."

I asked Bennett what his technical assistance group was doing. "The core of our effort is problem solving," he said.

"We're trying every strategy we can think of. We've done such elementary things as develop a booklet for higher-education admission policies that tells admissions people how to comply. Then we do more complicated things." One of the more complicated things, Bennett explained, was to strike a deal with the American Council on Education, an umbrella group that represents just about every institution of higher education in the country. The council is conducting workshops at colleges to explain the rules and suggest ways to comply. HEW turned over $100,000 toward the effort. Additional dollars were raised from private corporations. Besides these workshops, the council has established a hot line that institutions can call in order to get a speedy response to any question on compliance.

"Everyone is screaming about these rules, because they say they will cost too much," Bennett said. "We don't think they will cost too much. They will cost something. But there's a lot of money out there." He mentioned HUD grants. CETA money. Community block grants. Private foundations. Charities. Sources of funds, of course, are easier to list than to get money from. "The real bottom line in this," Bennett went on, "is that this is a civil-rights issue, and we don't think the courts will uphold that a person's rights can be abridged because the costs are too great."

HEW has already lost one important skirmish in the money area. Congress killed a $500 million application from HEW for barrier-removal funding. The agency suspects that the money out there will, in the end, prove inadequate. "What we're doing," Bennett explained, "is waiting now to see how everyone does. If money holds up things, as it may well, then we'll request some again from Congress."

Bennett pointed out that common sense is being used in order to get compliance. "It will be possible," he said, "for a city school system, within reasonable limits, to open up some but not all of its school buildings to the handicapped. Like maybe three elementary schools out of a dozen. That will save a lot of dollars. One thing we won't allow is a state system of ten campuses where only one campus is totally barrier-free. So that all handicapped students go there. We will not permit that. That is for the birds."

Bennett poked through a stack of papers on his desk. "Here's a letter I got this morning from a community college. It has two buildings close together, neither of which is accessible. It wants to build one elevator and a connecting bridge, saving it eighty thousand dollars from building two elevators. I believe this is an acceptable strategy."

Unofficially — around the halls and over the water coolers — HEW people suspect that satisfactory compliance is many years, perhaps decades, away. Officially, the word is only slightly rosier. I asked Bennett his sense of how compliance was coming along. "We don't really have a very good feel for this yet," he answered. "The regulations have not been in effect very long. We have studies under way now to find out what compliance has been like. Based on anecdotal evidence and nothing systematic, I think that higher education is moving a bit faster toward compliance than secondary education. I think that both varieties of education are moving along better than the health-care field — the hospitals, nursing homes, clinics, rehabilitation agencies. Employment is where most of the complaints are. Getting employers to alter their facilities will be easier than getting them to hire disabled workers." Bennett said that he had no hope of full compliance by deadline time. "That would be awfully naïve of me. This will go on for years and years and years. That is the nature of deeply imbedded prejudice."

Some original assumptions have already proved incorrect. One such article of faith was that making health-care facilities accessible would require little money or work, since they have already been set up to treat sick people. "That had turned out to be totally false," Bennett said. "Sometimes you will go into a hospital and nowhere in the whole damn place is a bathroom where a person in a wheelchair can go. Many hospitals won't hire disabled employees. The American Hospital Association said compliance would cost two billion dollars. That's bullshit, but the changes won't be inexpensive."

I asked Bennett how HEW was going to know whether satisfactory compliance has been achieved. Just how good was the mechanism for checking?

He explained that the civil-rights office was conducting so-called compliance reviews on a random basis. Twenty were scheduled in 1978, the first year they were done. Some take days, others weeks. Another hundred or so reviews, done each year, include handicapped compliance along with compliance on other forms of discrimination. Bennett said the office would like to increase the number of spot checks, but that that depended on the level of complaints, which must get first attention, and on staffing. His own office includes only fifteen people, but the number is expected to rise to seventy-two. His current budget is ten million dollars.

So complaints have been the best way to find out about lack of compliance. Regrettably, though, many disabled individuals don't know what their rights are. A lot of them shy away from public demonstrations of dissatisfaction. And places where the handicapped don't go provoke no complaints, and thus are ignored. That situation will probably get worse. "The basic mechanism," Bennett said, "is going to be voluntary compliance. We have no way to keep track of most places. I don't see how we will ever be able to."

Bennett pondered what he had said. A phone call came in. Then he had another thought. "I am willing to go out on a limb," he said. "I think that we will eventually win this battle. Just don't ask me when."

Near the end of my interview with Bennett, we were interrupted by an unexpected fire drill. Bennett looked flustered. The two of us gathered our things together and spurted after the flow of people streaming down the hallways. Procedure was to take the stairs down to the lobby. Since Bennett was in a wheelchair, we naturally headed for the elevator. We clambered in and dropped to the lobby level. The doors wouldn't open. "Oh shit," Bennett said. "They fixed them so they stay shut." We rode back upward in a silence broken only by the muffled whoosh of air and machinery. The doors still wouldn't budge. We sat in the dank elevator, comforted only by the fact that we had been told this was a drill. Finally, the doors sprang open.

"That was frightening," I said to Bennett as we shot out. "What would you have done if the fire had been real?"

His laugh blurted out like a rifle shot. "Why, burn up," he said.

The people who are on the battle lines, whose mission is to do the actual investigating of cases, are the equal opportunity specialists in the regional offices. One overcast day I went down to the Region II office for civil rights, headquartered near the Wall Street area of New York. Its considerable jurisdiction embraces New York, New Jersey, Puerto Rico, and the Virgin Islands. Just inside, a cluster of investigators stood in conference. Behind them were several couches on which were seated several handicapped people with grim faces. They sat in silence. Occasionally, an investigator would come and escort one of the people to his cubicle. All eyes would go up as they left. I spoke with half a dozen investigators, all of whom preferred anonymity.

They all seemed hardworking and dedicated, but were overwhelmed by a shortage of hours and by the hopelessness of having to cope with a constantly increasing caseload.

"All of our cases are trouble," a beefy, sloe-eyed man told me. "Civil rights is always trouble. I'm not going to get up on a soap box, but whenever you complain about civil rights, you put somebody out of joint. Everyone gives us a tussle. Plus, we're working with rules and regulations that are not all that clear. They have to be interpreted. And we have pressure on us to get these cases cleared up. So you don't have time to invent the wheel. One of our problems is getting information to and from the handicapped person. We just got a teletypewriter in here to communicate with the deaf. Sometimes the machine breaks down."

One of the other investigators, a weary-looking youngish man with a short beard, said, "These cases are tricky, because we are faced with the difficulty of defining whether the complainant is handicapped, before we even look into whether he was discriminated against. With race or sex, you don't have too much debate over who is black or who is a woman. You do with the handicapped. How do you deal with someone who has chronic lower-back pain and says he's been discriminated against because of it? We have to stop and ask: are we talking about a handicapped person? Maybe yes, and maybe no. We also have the problem of people who are not handicapped but who are perceived as being handicapped. Like someone may be seen as retarded, even though he's not. If the evidence suggests that the person has been perceived as handicapped, then we have cause for action in this office."

Another man, who looked more like the head of a swinging ad agency than an equal opportunity specialist, said, "I had a teacher who had had a radical mastectomy. Her classes changed from room to room, and she said she couldn't carry her books very well. Well, the difficulty was on the left side, and a cynical person might have said, 'Why don't you carry the books in your other arm?' But what we got was a nonrotating schedule for her. I must confess that that is more than I would have been content with. If the school had agreed to give her a cart to carry her books in, I might have to consider it. Whenever we can get a meeting of the minds, we have to consider the solution. You have to realize our sanctions. If people don't comply, we have to cut off federal funds. So we hurt the people we're trying to help. And we don't want to bankrupt anyone."

One investigator mentioned that a blind woman had called just the other day and said she was trying to visit her father in a hospital. The hospital refused to admit her, because of her Seeing Eye dog. "Now, perhaps dogs create a health problem there," the investigator said. "It's something we've got to do more homework on. It's a gray area."

I was told about another case involving a woman who had applied to a beauty school. She was admitted; however, the chemicals being used on the hair caused a severe allergic reaction. She was dismissed from the school. The person working on the case told me, "We're not sure whether that's a substantial enough effect on her to be a justified complaint. Because this woman can't go to this beauty school, or even to any beauty school, does that mean her life is affected in some meaningful way? The case has been sent to Washington for a policy ruling on it."

"The complaints cover the whole spectrum," said a cheerful, impish-looking investigator. "You hear of a new one every day. Like one I just had: a handicapped person who claimed he was being discriminated against in taking law school admission tests. Whenever he turns his head, his eyes lose focus and he can't see anything for a few minutes. So when he finishes reading a question and turns to mark down the answer, his vision clouds up and he takes far too long to do the tests to get a decent score. Now, should he get more time? What is reasonable? Would waiving the test be reasonable? I never heard of this handicap before, so how do I know? If someone has a problem with bowel movements and a bathroom is across the hall in his dormitory, is that reasonable accommodation or should he have a bathroom off his room? These are gray areas."

All the investigators I spoke with readily admitted that these were the toughest discrimination cases they have handled. They had no precedents to go on. They had no statistics. One of them said, "The investigator has to ask the right questions, be creative, and have some luck. Sometimes you can sense in your gut after a while when something is rotten. But sensing in your gut and actually being able to prove it on paper are different things. So many cases could go either way. You can't just flip a coin and say that's it. At times, though, that's what you feel like you're doing."

Government people were absolutely certain that laws could only do so much. Discrimination inevitably leaves lingering damage. Too many people, I was told again and again, are waiting around with impossible expectations.

13

Shooting across the Brooklyn Bridge and then thundering deep into the bowels of Brooklyn, the F train was noisy and uncomfortable. Somebody was playing a shoulder-strapped Panasonic — turned up, blaring. Soul music. I got off at Fifteenth Street in Park Slope and walked the couple of blocks to the house of John Kenny. Past the Samler's Theater, out of business, soon to be reborn as a hardware store. I was dampened by a little spattering of rain. The house was unattractive, and garbage was heaped up out front. It was a creaky, two-family brownstone. The Kennys lived on the bottom floor, behind a thick black steel door. In the upstairs windows of the houses across the street, women sat quietly smoking.

John was at the library, cramming for an upcoming exam, and I was let in by his father, John Sr., a burly, stoop-shouldered man, recently retired as an inspector for the city's water resources department. He flashed a hospitable smile and extended his hand. The living room had a scarcely inhabited look. But in John's bedroom, an anarchy of records and books and bedsheets, we barely had room to move. A mechanical lift dominated one side, and a toilet was propped up next to the bed. On a nightstand rested a phone with a headset attached to it. A poster tacked on the wall said, "Bring Back the Bullmoose Party."

I was directed to a seat in the living room, and goaded into accepting a big chunk of cake and tea. John's father was drinking a Dr Pepper while watching a band of television Indians whose savage whoops were drowned out by car horns crashing through the apartment and probably rattling the china.

He spoke in a swift, staccato manner of speech. "Our boy has had it rough," he said with certainty. "All these people are looking for somebody to make fun of, some poor fellow who didn't have the luck they had. But he's stuck it out. I figure he's going to do okay. I sure think he'll do okay."

His mother, Catherine, a plain-looking, sunny woman in a rumpled house dress, burst in. "John's doing fairly good now," she said. "He's learning that he has no reason to feel peculiar. He's figuring out where he's at."

John was born a few blocks away in 1950. When he was five, he went with his parents to a friend's party. He remembers having a great time. They came home late, and he scurried off to his room to go to bed. Between the door and the bed, he fell down. He was a little surprised; he hadn't tripped over anything. Then he tried to get up. He couldn't budge. He got very scared and cried out for his parents.

The polio was diagnosed right away in the hospital. But it didn't seem to be terribly severe. John was released with a brace on the right leg that climbed to his hip, and he could bound along pretty well with a crutch. When he was eleven, he had an operation to release a tendon that was stiffening up in the right leg. That worked out all right. Then when he turned thirteen, an awful metamorphosis began to take place. He started to have trouble climbing stairs. He would be short of breath and beads of sweat would erupt on his forehead. He had another operation to free the heel cord in the left foot. The walking, though, was still strenuous, and he returned to the hospital for a lengthy string of tests to figure out what the trouble was. The tests turned up nothing. More and more, however, he was riding in a wheelchair rather than walking with his crutch. When he was fifteen he entered a state rehabilitation hospital in West Havistrod, New York. His parents, not to mention John himself, were desperate to know what was wrong. "I kept saying to the doctors, 'Now what am I supposed to tell people when they ask what exactly is wrong with John?' " his mother remembered. "Am I supposed to say, 'Well, we have no idea. Just something mysterious.' " In the hospital in West Havistrod, John couldn't rise out of the wheelchair at all. The same tests were administered. Nobody really knows why, but this time they showed muscular dystrophy. No doubt remained. John would never walk again. When he was told the news, he plunged into a deep depression. He considered suicide. He was too scared to kill himself, though, and he began to think maybe some miracle cure would be invented if he just hung in there long enough. But long lonely months of ugly nightmares passed before he got over his despair.

He returned home when he was eighteen. His parents were living in the house they now occupy, only they were settled on the second floor, up two steep flights of stairs. John could get outside only by being hoisted down the stairs. He got out maybe once or twice a month. Still, he felt he was ready to rebuild an identity. He enrolled in Long Island University, studying journalism, using an intercom system hooked up across phone lines, between the classrooms and the Kenny living room. It worked fine, except with one teacher, who wouldn't stand for any machines in his class. "Out, out, out," he screamed when he spotted a maintenance man wiring up the device. John thought the man was merely sensitive to the intercom, until a blind student phoned him and told him that he had encountered unimaginable problems right in the classroom. John threatened to sue the teacher. The dean intervened and John completed the course. He plugged away at school for several more years, in spite of disheartening setbacks. Four times he was hobbled by awful colds and had to return to the hospital. He got frustrated and depressed at how long his education was taking; he didn't really feel part of the class, huddled in his living room listening to an intercom. So he dropped out and spent two years moping around and feeling sorry for himself. When he was twenty-two, his parents bought the house they were living in and moved downstairs. He had freedom then, and could go outside and roll around in his wheelchair. The feel of it energized him the way someone else his age might have been excited by a first chance to drive a car. Friends harped on him to get his act together and make something of his life. So what if he was in a chair, he could still do something. He finally mustered up the courage to enroll in a paralegal program for adult students at LIU. He agreed, for the first time, to attend in person. A modified bus picks him up, along with other disabled students, and shuttles them back and forth to the campus.

The mustard-colored bus slid up to the curb outside and swung slowly into a parking spot big enough to handle an Allied moving van. John clacked down the ramp. An attendant helped him into the living room. He jockeyed into a position where he could see me comfortably, smiled, and said hello. He has a plump face and wavy rust-colored hair conventionally cut. He needs to breathe through a scuba-diver type respirator. His lungs gave up on him three years ago. He wore threadbare pants, a faded denim shirt and a gold sweater. He said the air conditioning in the library had been on high. "I thought the Ice Age had returned."

John was approaching thirty. He had never held a job. He once contemplated starting a van service to transport disabled people. "It sounded great. I thought I'd be richer than hell. Then I put the numbers down on paper." The figures showed that he would need twenty thousand dollars in start-up money. He had none. Briefly, he flirted with the idea of a mail-order business as the ticket to success, but gave up on that, too. He has never lived outside of hospitals or away from his family. I asked him about that. I had talked to many people as disabled as he was who were out leading independent lives. Why wasn't he?

After a short silence, he murmured, "Just scared." John has a high-pitched laugh, almost a giggle — a surprising sound to come out of a large, cello-shaped man, and he laughed now. But he seemed to be skirting the question. It didn't make sense that he could simply be a spineless coward. I pressed him further.

He hesitated, thinking back. He did not seem to want to rake up the embers. At last, he said he almost moved out a couple of years ago. He had met another handicapped man about his age when he was in Goldwater Hospital for his respiratory problem. The man's name was Michael Cioffi. When he was twenty-three, he was driving to Massachusetts with the woman he was going to marry when he began to feel feverish. He pulled onto the shoulder and asked his fiancée to take the wheel. He got worse, and urged that they stop at a hospital. He collapsed as he walked in the door. He never walked again. An odd virus, for inexplicable reasons, had attacked him. He was left permanently paralyzed. His fiancée insisted on going through with the wedding, but he was Italian, and had been raised to believe that the man was the breadwinner in the house, no exceptions, and he couldn't picture himself as anybody's husband.

His parents had died long ago. He either had to live in the hospital or go out on his own. He badly wanted to leave the hospital, so he approached John with the idea of the two of them getting an apartment together. "I could see his point of view right away. I thought it would be a good thing to take care of myself and see if I could fit my life together." John was discharged from the hospital, but he frequently bantered with Michael on the phone about their plans. Then Michael began to get sicker. Some days, he didn't get out of bed at all. John figured it would surely pass.

One evening, John was lazily watching the news on television. The hospitals in New York had come under an awful budget crunch, and Mayor Beame was threatening to shut down some of them. Patients and hospital staff were kicking up a storm. The news switched to a report on a patient who, the reporter said, had been terribly morose about the prospect of Goldwater Hospital closing down and leaving him stranded with nowhere to go (though, in fact, the patient had been no more despondent about this than any other patient). He was paralyzed and had no family, the report went on. It might have been this depression that triggered his death that morning. The patient's name: Michael Cioffi.

John was shattered. No one had notified him. "I looked at the set and felt pain. I broke into a cold sweat. I couldn't believe it. It was all the worse, because I saw myself in Michael. We were so much alike. Life had dealt him the same hand. He was paralyzed. He had the same respiratory problem. He was twenty-seven. I was twenty-five. I got to thinking that it was really unfair that somebody so young should die. Was this what was in store for me?"

John wondered. He is still wondering that today. He was spooked and began to abandon the dream of an independent life. He was sullen about Michael's death for months. He didn't finally come to grips with it until he began to see a social worker regularly and talked it out. "I was feeling trapped like a fly in a spiderweb."

John began to cough. He called his father and asked for a drink of water. His father lightfooted it into the room with a glass that had a straw poking out of it. John quaffed it down. "Now drink it slow," his father said. He acted like a working dentist.

His throat relieved, John said, "So much of the time, being able-bodied seems something you can't survive without. And if you're handicapped, you can never believe in what you will be — you don't ever really believe in what you are. So you dream about magical transformations."

John's presence can be hard on the family. Two attendants alternate caring for him forty hours a week. But they aren't around at night or on weekends. Also living at home is a sister, Grace, who's nineteen. Auburn-haired, large-boned, she works as a teller in the Independent Savings Bank. His paunchy, silent brother, Gregory, twenty, is studying law enforcement at John Jay College. He works on the auxiliary police force and hopes to get into police work full time. All the Kennys are direct and hospitable. John's family takes turns getting him up and putting him to bed, and otherwise assisting him. They are sometimes pooped from the work. When John gets touchy, as he is apt to, the rest of the family "tells me to drown myself." Occasionally haggles erupt over who will put him to bed. "Oh, I put him to bed yesterday," someone will say. "No, I did it yesterday — you do it tonight."

"John, I think, will get his own place when he feels he's ready," his mother allowed.

"There's no rush," his father said. "Whenever he wants to, we'll be sure to help him."

"I know my parents aren't getting any younger," John cut in. "Every day I see them getting older. I wonder when I should relieve the burden."

"I wouldn't say it's a burden," his mother barked.

"It's no burden," his father said.

"Oh, I know," John said. He clasped his hands and gazed across the room. Across his face flew a quick, thin smile.

In many respects, John embodies the fright so many disabled people feel about setting up a life of their own in a world that is still not ready for them. They are in a bind: they can't comfort themselves, and society won't show them the way. John is essentially where he has been for the last decade. He is frozen in time. He doesn't do much. He has few friends. He doesn't date girls; he looks on the prospect as futile. Once a month, he'll go to the ball game or to Belmont Park to watch the horses run. He hardly ever takes in a movie or play. Money is a limitation. Getting a New York van company to carry him to Yankee Stadium socks him for thirty-five dollars. He has to book it three weeks to several months in advance. He eats out no more than once or twice a year. "I'm comfortable eating at home," he said.

Does he have any joy in his life? I wondered. I asked him whether he felt he had accepted his condition. He is a remarkably honest person. If John Kenny had ever cut down a cherry tree, he would probably have reported it without being asked.

"Not really," he answered. "I think I will always be bitter. I think a lot about what life would be like if I were able-bodied. By now, I'd probably be married, maybe have kids, have a job, have a car. I don't really know what kind of job. I know I wouldn't want to work in an office, the nine-to-five routine. Maybe that comes from having had to sit in a chair all my life. I might be in politics. I like politics a lot."

What did he imagine his life would be like five years from now? I asked.

"I guess I don't really like to think that far in advance," he said. "There could be more problems. Getting old worries me. Not the prospect of getting old, but getting old with disability frightens me. I don't know if my life will be better or worse. Changes are coming for the handicapped. But very, very slowly. This is a land of plenty for the healthy. Maybe a land of too much. But it's still a land of barriers for the disabled. Barriers. Barriers. Barriers. So much out there is working against me." He shook his head, and started to jiggle gently the control switch on his power wheelchair.

The cool spring air began to penetrate his plaid sweater, and John bunched his shoulders and bowed his head over his immobile body. Outside, a baby was squalling. In the other room, I could hear John's mother doing the dishes. After the longest pause, John nodded gradually and said, "I want to get out. I really do. I want to prove that I can hold a job. I want to prove that I can live alone. I'm waiting for society to change some more, for it to fix itself up and be okay for people like me. A friend of mine came up with an analogy of my life, and I guess it's not that far off base. He said I was like a shipwrecked sailor on a deserted island. I know the ships are coming for me, but I don't know when. So I just wait. I just wait for the ships to come."

Appendix

A LISTING OF ORGANIZATIONS FOR THE HANDICAPPED

Literally thousands of organizations deal with the problems of the handicapped. What follows is a selection of some of the larger and more prominent groups, sources for advice and information. The list includes government agencies as well as private associations.

American Coalition of Citizens with Disabilities Inc.
1346 Connecticut Avenue, N.W., Suite 817
Washington, D.C. 20036

> *A national organization that speaks for all disabilities. It acts chiefly as a lobbying force to insure that legislation affecting the handicapped is enforced and to push for new laws.*

American Council of the Blind
1211 Connecticut Avenue, N.W., Suite 506
Washington, D.C. 20036

> *An advocate for legislation and services for the blind.*

American Foundation for the Blind
15 West 16th Street
New York, New York 10011

> *Works to help the blind adapt to living independently.*

Architectural and Transportation Barriers Compliance Board
Office of Human Development
U.S. Department of Health, Education and Welfare
330 C Street, S.W.
Washington, D.C. 20201

> *Monitors compliance with parts of the Rehabilitation Act related to architectural and transportation barriers.*

Bureau of Education for the Handicapped
Office of Education
U.S. Department of Health, Education and Welfare
Donohue Building
Washington, D.C. 20202

> *Funds special education programs and trains teachers to work with the handicapped.*

Center for Independent Living
2539 Telegraph Avenue
Berkeley, California 94704

> *An organization made up largely of disabled individuals. Works for the integration of handicapped people into the community.*

Closer Look
National Information Center for the Handicapped
1201 16th Street, N.W., Suite 607 E
Washington, D.C. 20036

> *Furnishes information about the education of the disabled.*

Council for Exceptional Children
1920 Association Drive
Reston, Virginia 22091

> *Supports research and training aimed at improving the education of handicapped children. Works with specialists who serve these children.*

Disability Rights Center
1346 Connecticut Avenue, N.W.
Washington, D.C. 20036

> *Advocacy group working to insure fair treatment of the disabled by employers.*

Disabled American Veterans
National Headquarters
P.O. Box 14301
Cincinnati, Ohio 45214

> *Lobbies for improved benefits for disabled veterans.*

Human Resources Center
Willets Road
Albertson, New York 11507

> *Specializes in rehabilitation and special education of severely handicapped people.*

Mainstream Inc.
200 15th Street, N.W.
Washington, D.C. 20005

> *Lobbies for employment of the handicapped. Operates a "Call for Compliance" hotline.*

Muscular Dystrophy Association of America Inc.
810 Seventh Avenue
New York, New York 10019

> *Promotes research seeking cures for muscular dystrophy and related diseases.*

National Arts and the Handicapped Information Service
Box 2040
Grand Central Station
New York, New York 10017

> *Provides information to make arts programs and facilities accessible to the handicapped.*

National Association for Retarded Citizens
2709 Avenue E East
Box 6109
Arlington, Texas 76011

> *Promotes research about and training for the mentally retarded.*

National Association of the Deaf
814 Thayer Avenue
Silver Spring, Maryland 20910

> *Fosters research into deafness and acts as an advocacy group for the deaf.*

National Association of the Physically Handicapped
2819 Terrace Road, S.E., Apt. A-465
Washington, D.C. 20020

> *Works to further the cause of all physically disabled people.*

National Blindness Information Center (National Federation of the Blind)
1346 Connecticut Avenue, N.W.
Washington, D.C. 20036

> *Circulates information relating to the blind. Has a hotline number.*

National Center for Law and the Handicapped
1235 North Eddy Street
South Bend, Indiana 46617

> *Fosters enforcement of legislation affecting the handicapped.*

National Easter Seal Society for Crippled
Children and Adults
2023 West Ogden Avenue
Chicago, Illinois 60612

> *Promotes research and funds services for all varieties of disabled individuals.*

National Foundation/March of Dimes
1275 Mamaroneck Avenue
White Plains, New York 10605

> *Mainly encourages research into the prevention of birth defects.*

National Multiple Sclerosis Society
205 East 42nd Street
New York, New York 10010

> *Fosters research on multiple sclerosis.*

National Paraplegia Foundation
333 North Michigan Avenue
Chicago, Illinois 60601

> *Supports research into spinal cord injuries.*

National Rehabilitation Association
1522 K Street, N.W.
Washington, D.C. 20005

> *Disseminates information among professionals who work in rehabilitating the disabled.*

Office for Civil Rights
Office of the Secretary
U.S. Department of Health, Education and Welfare
330 Independence Avenue, S.W.
Washington, D.C. 20201

> *Monitors compliance with the civil rights regulations of the Rehabilitation Act for HEW. Coordinates the enforcement administered by all federal agencies on civil rights matters.*

Office of Federal Contracts Compliance Programs
Employment Standards Administration
U.S. Department of Labor
600 D Street, S.W.
Washington, D.C. 20201

> *Enforces the employment provisions of the Rehabilitation Act.*

Office of Handicapped Individuals
Office for Human Development
U.S. Department of Health, Education and Welfare
200 Independence Avenue, S.W.
Washington, D.C. 20201

> *Furnishes a wide variety of information on programs for the handicapped.*

President's Committee on Employment of the Handicapped
1111 20th Street, N.W., Suite 636
Washington, D.C. 20036

> *Provides information about the employment of the handicapped.*

Rehabilitation Services Administration
Office of Human Development
U.S. Department of Health, Education and Welfare
330 C Street, S.W.
Washington, D.C., 20201

> *Funds research into rehabilitation of the disabled. Trains counselors and funds vocational training programs.*

United Cerebral Palsy Association Inc.
66 East 34th Street
New York, New York 10016

> *Deals with a wide scope of problems experienced by people with cerebral palsy.*

Veterans Administration
Washington, D.C. 20420

> *Administers programs for disabled veterans. Also, its research centers are among the principal developers and evaluators of devices to assist the disabled.*